William Morris in Oxford

William Morris in Oxford

The Campaigning Years, 1879–1895

—————————

TONY PINKNEY

Grosmont

Published in Great Britain in 2007
by illuminati books, Glyndŵr, Grosmont, NP7 8EP
www.illuminatibooks.co.uk

Designed and typeset by illuminati
Printed in the EU by Short Run Press, Exeter

A catalogue record for this book is available from the British Library

ISBN 978 0 9555918 0 8

To Mum and Dad,
with all my love

'Nay,' said I, 'I come not from heaven but from Essex'
A Dream of John Ball

Contents

Abbreviations

Writings by William Morris and Associates

CW = *The Collected Works of William Morris*, edited by May Morris, 24 volumes, 1910–15 (London: Routledge/Thoemmes Press, 1992)

CL = *The Collected Letters of William Morris*, edited by Norman Kelvin, 4 volumes (Princeton, NJ: Princeton University Press, 1984–96)

AWS = *William Morris: Artist Writer Socialist*, edited by May Morris, 2 volumes, 1936 (Tokyo: Editions Synapse, 2005)

PW = *Political Writings: Contributions to 'Justice' and 'Commonweal' 1883–1890*, edited by Nicholas Salmon (Bristol: Thoemmes Press, 1994)

J = *Journalism: Contributions to 'Commonweal' 1885–1890*, edited by Nicholas Salmon (Bristol: Thoemmes Press, 1996)

SPAB 1 = Society for the Protection of Ancient Buildings archive on Magdalen Bridge, Oxford

SPAB 2 = Society for the Protection of Ancient Buildings archive on St Mary's Church, Oxford

WMC = *William Morris Collection: Part Three: Archives of the Socialist League, 1884–1891*, microfilm (Reading: Research Publications, 1989)

Newspapers and Journals 1879–1895

C = *Commonweal*

JOJ = *Jackson's Oxford Journal*

OC = *Oxford Chronicle*

OCUJ = *Oxford and Cambridge Undergraduate's Journal*
OM = *Oxford Magazine*
OT = *Oxford Times*
T = *The Times*
PMG = *Pall Mall Gazette*

Other Oxford Sources

HUO = *The History of the University of Oxford*, Volume VII: *Nineteenth-Century Oxford*, edited by M.G. Brock and M.C. Curthoys (Oxford: Clarendon Press, Part 1 1997; Part 2 2000)

Introduction

[P]laces I feel myself impelled to speak of, a place, a second home;
the city of Oxford.

William Morris, July 1881 (*CL*, II, 58)

The question has been asked, 'is the new Oxford movement to be a
Socialistic one?'

Oxford Magazine (21 November 1883, 384)

Oxford – both city and university – was always a profoundly
significant place to William Morris. In August 1881 he wrote to
Georgiana Burne-Jones: 'A kind of terror always falls upon me as I near
it; indignation at wanton or rash changes mingles curiously in me with
all that I remember I have lost since I was a lad and dwelling there; not
the least of losses the recognition that I didn't know in those days what
a gain it was to be there' (*CL*, II, 60). So intense did this Oxonian terror
eventually become for Morris that according to his friend and publisher,
F.S. Ellis, 'in later years ... it was with difficulty he could be persuaded
to go thither' (Ellis, 620); and May Morris confirms this, describing
Oxford as 'the city loved of old, the city he never visited willingly now'
(*AWS*, I, 89). Morris himself once made the point in comic rather than
tragic mode, declaring that he would never enter the city again 'unless
they make me drunk at the station' (Ashley and Saunders, 5).

Born in 1834, William Morris had been an undergraduate at Exeter College from 1853 to 1855. He may have been dissatisfied with the formal education on offer, but here he met his lifetime's friend, Edward Burne-Jones, and, through Burne-Jones, the Birmingham contingent of Charles Faulkner, William Fulford, Cormell Price and Richard Dixon, with whom (among others) he put together *The Oxford and Cambridge Magazine* in 1856. In that same year Morris was articled to the architect G.E. Street, whose offices were in Beaumont Street, Oxford; and here he met another long-term friend and ally, Philip Webb. In 1857, after following Street to London, Morris was back in Oxford, enthusiastically decorating the Oxford Union building as part of a team organised by Dante Gabriel Rossetti. It was in this year that he met Jane Burden, who had grown up in lowly circumstances in Holywell Street, and on 26 April 1859 he and Jane were married at St Michael's Church, Oxford.

Oxford, then, had in these years (sometimes despite itself) been to Morris a place of youthful exuberance, of expanding intellectual, artistic, personal and sexual horizons, and his fondness for it is signalled by his return visits in later years. The Morris and Burne-Jones families spent the summer in lodgings in the city in 1867, teaming up with Charles Faulkner, who was now a Fellow of University College. Whitsun 1875 saw Morris and Burne-Jones back in the city again. They met John Ruskin there, who, as we shall see, was to play a significant role in some of Morris's later Oxford campaigns; but the visit seems mostly to have been a recovery of undergraduate male camaraderie: 'Mr Morris and Mr Faulkner and I almost lived on the river, Sunday and Monday', Burne-Jones later recalled (Burne-Jones, I, 58). In mid-June of that year Morris returned to take his M.A. degree, though it isn't clear how much enthusiasm for his alma mater this actually indicates; for George Bernard Shaw later remarked that 'the only item in his past expenditure [Morris] thoroughly grudged was the twenty pounds his Oxford degree of Master of Arts had cost him' (*AWS*, II, ix).

Morris also sustained a professional as well as personal relationship with Oxford during this period. His decorative firm Morris, Marshall, Faulkner and Co. – reorganised as Morris and Co. from 1875 – provided stained glass for the St Edmund Hall chapel in 1864–5, the Vyner Memorial window and three others for Christ Church Cathedral in the

1870s, and it redecorated the Oxford Union roof in an attractive design of leaves and red flowers in 1875. This professional decorative relationship – no doubt with a good deal of nostalgic personal feeling mixed in too – culminates in the great 'Adoration of the Magi' tapestry commissioned by Exeter College in 1886 and finally completed in 1890. It is one of the minor myths of Morris's relationship to Oxford that he gave this tapestry to Exeter gratis, out of old collegial affection. In fact, however, he charged the college the hefty sum of £525 for it, thus making back many times over the £20 his M.A. degree had cost.

Oxford University, in the person of James Thursfield writing on behalf of Convocation, showed its recognition of Morris's growing literary achievement by inviting him to stand for election to the Professorship of Poetry in 1877, although this was an honour its recipient declined, after much hard thought. In extending the invitation the University was no doubt honouring the author of *The Life and Death of Jason* (1867) and *The Earthly Paradise* (1868–70), but by 1877 this was an identity Morris was already leaving far behind. He had spent the year heavily involved in the political agitation conducted by the Eastern Question Association, and had embarked on a major campaign of cultural agitation too, by founding the Society for the Protection of Ancient Buildings in March. Morris now had a public mission and message; he certainly wanted to lecture to his contemporaries, but not about poetry. Declining the Oxford invitation gave him time and space to address other, broader issues; and in December 1877 he gave his first public lecture, on 'The Decorative Arts', and his first political speech, at an anti-war meeting of the Eastern Question Association, both in London.

As Morris reinvented himself as a cultural and political activist, so his relationship to Oxford necessarily changed. It was no longer the place of carefree memories and happy river trips, but a forum where the issues that absorbed him so passionately were being fought out, where influential opinion-makers could be reached and young minds shaped and inspired. It would not be long before the energetic public speaker Morris was becoming in the late 1870s would turn his attention to his old university and attempt to intervene forcefully in its debates; and when he did so this would be an altogether more serious matter than

Rossetti's 'jovial campaign' of the Oxford Union decorations in 1857 (MacCarthy, 129). Whatever personal 'terror' afflicted Morris about Oxford in his later years would need to be fought down, clearly, in order that he could get at this crucial, opinion-forming audience.

This book charts William Morris's Oxford interventions; it tells the story of his mature relationship with his former university and its city (though the old fondness and nostalgia never vanish entirely, naturally), and does so by re-creating the nine lectures and speeches that he gave at Oxford from November 1879 to October 1895. One of these, 'Art under Plutocracy', is by common consent one of Morris's very finest lectures and around it, as I shall demonstrate, much scholarly myth has accreted. Two others also appear in the *Collected Works* (though one of these has not been recognised as an Oxford lecture by Morris scholars from May Morris onwards), and the other six have either been reprinted only in portions or not at all. In such cases I have reconstructed them as best I can from contemporary journalistic accounts or, in one case, transcribed the text from Morris's manuscript in the British Library. And certainly none of these lectures and speeches has previously been considered as a self-contained set, as part of Morris's urgent campaign to win over his old university on both architectural and political issues. To help us see them more firmly as such, I have reconstructed the Oxford political context in which Morris was intervening and have traced the practical effects his lectures and speeches had there.

Most previous commentators on the issue of Morris and Oxford have concentrated on the question of what Oxford gave to Morris: how its cultural treasures – medieval manuscripts as well as ancient buildings – inspired him, or how contemporary intellectual influences – Carlyle, Ruskin, Kingsley, even the *Builder* – shaped him formatively there as an undergraduate, or how through the Oxford School of historians (E.A. Freeman, J.R. Green, Thorold Rogers) it guided his thinking about the medieval period in later life. My focus, however, will be not what Oxford gave to Morris but what he, in his mature years, gave to *it*, what he strove to make happen there, how he aspired to become in his turn a formative intellectual influence on new generations of students. Unlike Matthew Arnold, who was Professor of Poetry from 1857 to 1867, or John Ruskin, who was Slade Professor of Art at the university from

1869 to 1878 and again from 1883 to 1885, Morris never had a formal position at Oxford. Yet the organisations which he either created or attached himself to in his mature years – the Society for the Protection of Ancient Buildings, the Democratic Federation, the Socialist League – all aspired to establish themselves in the city in one way or another and to have a continuing impact upon students, dons and townspeople. Morris, then, in the story I aim to tell, is not the passive beneficiary of Oxford, an eighteen-year-old *tabula rasa* scrawled gratefully over by the cultural riches of the place, but rather an active agent of change, an extraordinarily energetic polemicist and lecturer who intends, if he can, to reshape profoundly the history of the university and the city, to create – in a term that was current at the time – a 'new Oxford movement'. This book narrates the story of those interventions and measures the degree of success they had at Oxford, within Morris's lifetime and beyond.

We should certainly see Morris's decision to rent Kelmscott Manor from June 1871 as part of the story I am telling here. True, its acquisition pre-dates his new identity as political and cultural activist by six years, but it creates a narrative and spatial structure which will be determinant for that later career from 1878 onwards: to get from Kelmscott House in London, the dystopian and Cobbettian 'wen' of Victorian capitalism, to a utopian idyll in the English countryside, one has to pass *through* Oxford. Morris could always call in to Oxford on his way down to Lechlade by train, either to buy a boat there or for a brisk spot of architectural tourism (*CL*, I, 175; IV, 214); and he enacted the passage from London through Oxford to Kelmscott on the grand scale in his two journeys by boat from one end of the Thames to the other in 1880 and 1881. He would perform it again, metaphorically rather than literally, in the river journey of Dick, Clara, Guest and Ellen in his utopia, *News from Nowhere*, in 1890; and he aspires to enact it in another sense – political rather than spatial – in the Oxford campaigns I examine in this volume.

Kelmscott was close enough to Oxford for some of Morris's spirited younger artist friends to do the journey out there by bicycle in the 1890s; and for Morris himself to have the Manor and village as a utopian reference point outside Oxford from which he could none the less be in touch with the city and university's affairs was a familiar nineteenth-century model. We might think of Matthew Arnold's Scholar-Gipsy, that other 'idle singer of an empty day', who is alienated from the university yet perpetually wandering the Oxfordshire countryside, as if the utopian 'spark from heaven' could only fall while he was still somehow in contact with the city in which he can no longer bear to live. Or if Arnold's shy scholar seems too quiescent a parallel for William Morris, we might think of John Ruskin's various Oxford campaigns from the 1850s onwards. In the words of Ruskin's best biographer Tim Hilton, Oxford 'began to appear as a city in which many of his hopes might be realized', and yet he 'developed his aversion to staying in Oxford. In 1857 he lived in a rented cottage in Cowley, three miles outside the city; in 1861 he stayed at Beckley, six miles away; and when he was elected as Slade Professor in 1871 he took up lodgings in a public house in Abingdon, six miles away in the other direction' (Hilton, 216, 224). The would-be reformer can thus not lodge within the city itself; it is as if to do so would fatally compromise his power of intervention, would immerse him too much in the grubby details of municipal or university politics. Rather does his base outside the city open him to the possibilities of prophetic inspiration, as with the Scholar-Gipsy – a prophetic afflatus which once had Morris describing himself, in 1887, as 'the maniac of Kelmscott' (Sharp 1999, 51). Thus inspired he can, like Ruskin and Morris and unlike the Scholar-Gipsy, venture back amidst the dreaming spires to fight the good fight against the innumerable foes of the day.

Too much of the writing about Morris and Oxford has been biographical and anecdotal. It is only Raymond Williams, who himself meditated deeply on the relation between Oxford University and a wider class politics in his novel *Second Generation* (1964), who has grasped the structural position of Oxford in Morris's later thought. This book should therefore be seen as the expansion of a pregnant remark in Williams's *Culture and Society*: 'Oxford was for him a test-case, on the issue whether culture could be preserved from commercialism by isolating it' (Williams, 151). Morris certainly accepted the general Ruskinian principle that the culture of a period could not be separated from the quality of its wider social life; as he insists in 'The Aims of Art', there is a 'connection between industrial slavery and the degradation of the arts' (*CW*, XXIII, 89). But it was one thing to know this in theory, quite another to witness it in practice; and to see his old university, for all its immense cultural prestige and privilege, cave in time after time to what he often called the 'Century of Commerce' was a bitter lesson indeed. Oxford may have regarded itself as a Tennysonian 'palace of art' immune from the economic philistinism of its day, but to the later Morris this kind of stance was precisely a symptom of capitulation to capitalism, not any kind of challenge to it. The question for Morris then became whether his campaigning in Oxford could move beyond defensive rearguard architectural actions into the more active promotion of general social change.

The Reverend Stopford Brooke, author of a sensitive study of Morris's poetry in 1908, once remarked, apropos of J.W. Mackail's biography, that no Oxford man could understand Morris's personality, unless after twenty reincarnations (cited in *AWS*, I, 80). Since my own involvement with Morris's work dates from my Oxford years I hope that I have not fallen foul of this judgement, though anyway my focus here is on Morris's campaigns rather than on his personality. Such Morrisian understanding as I can muster certainly owes much to the Oxford friends who shared the campaigns launched by Oxford English Limited (OEL) and its journal *News from Nowhere* between 1986 and 1991. Foremost among them were Terry Eagleton, Robin Gable, Ken Hirschkop and Craig Dowler, though Pete Higginson, Ros Ballaster, Sally Ledger, Carol Watts, Alastair Williams, Ben Morgan, Terry Murphy, Tetsuo Maruko, Stephanie Flood and Giles Goodland also played important roles; Steve Regan, David Norbrook and Paul Hamilton were supportive presences too. I was also lucky early in my Oxford days to have had the good company of Professor Tatsuo Tokoo, his wife Yoko and their daughter Ayako. Pamela White and Alison Easton have been precious Lancaster friends who have helped keep this project on course during rocky times, and Karen Young and Dina Lew have been forces for good in its later stages. Brian Ingram has helped greatly too, on and off the golf course. Lucy Morton of illuminati has been polyphiloprogenitive in suggestions for improvement.

I am also grateful to several good Morrisian friends for their sustained encouragement and help over the years: Peter Faulkner and

Ruth Levitas have been particularly crucial here. Several librarians and archivists have been especially helpful as I have chased the more arcane material I have required for this book: my particular thanks go to Jenny Brine of Lancaster University Library and Miss Greenhill, archivist of the Society for the Protection of Ancient Buildings (which Morris once memorably called 'the most prudent society in all England', *CW*, XXII, 234). I also owe a great debt to Eugene LeMire's bibliography of contemporary accounts of Morris's lectures in his *The Unpublished Lectures of William Morris*. Though I have found some additional Oxford sources which LeMire does not list there, I could not have even begun this book without the help of the prodigious feat of scholarship that his own bibliography represents.

It has been exciting to work on this study of Morris in Oxford during the years in which my son Justin, who was born at the John Radcliffe Hospital in 1986, is himself a student there, reading Physics at New College (in the cloisters of which Morris's beloved St Mary's statues were to end up). His early years in Oxford, as baby and toddler, were among the happiest ones that his mother Makiko Minow and I shared together. Justin has contributed much technical help in the production of this volume, and its dedication, to his grandparents in Southend-on-Sea, records my deepest debt of all. There is a long devoted record of love and support from them, which goes very much further back than my recent use of Southend as a base to commute to London for British Library research for this and other Morrisian projects. So: thanks to Dad for lifts to the railway station, and to Mum for sumptuous packed lunches, among so many other more precious things!

TP, September 2007

ONE

St Mark's at the Sheldonian, 1879

B uilt in 1664–69, the Sheldonian Theatre is still one of Oxford's
most striking buildings. It was the first major commission of the
ambitious young architect Christopher Wren, who was then Professor of
Astronomy at the University and who based his design on the Roman
Theatre of Marcellus. In the late seventeenth century the Sheldonian
served for a while as the University printing press, but its main use
today is for the conferring of degrees. For the rest of the year it is
available for lectures and concerts, and visitors are permitted to climb
to the cupola for views of the city centre. The views may not be as
commanding as those from St Mary's Church spire, but one has an
agreeable sense of being held within the architecture of the city rather
than lording over it from above.

On the afternoon of Saturday 15 November 1879 the Sheldonian
Theatre was alive with activity. Rectors, Wardens, Provosts and Principals of Oxford colleges and halls had filed into the building; a whole
panoply of the University's most distinguished professors had joined
them; churchmen were there in force; nationally known artists had
turned up; the ladies of Oxford were there too; and a fair number of
undergraduates swelled the ranks of the gathering, presumably keen
to admire the assembled celebrities. This was an impressive muster
of the great and the good of Oxford University at what the *Cambridge*

Review mischievously termed 'an Artistic Indignation meeting'. Its chair was Henry George Liddell, Dean of Christ Church College from 1855 onwards, Vice-Chancellor of the University between 1870 and 1874, and father of Lewis Carroll's Alice – an academic 'whose stately presence is enough in itself to lend dignity to any meeting', as the *Cambridge Review* rather chillingly put it (19 November 1879, 90).

Much Artistic Indignation was indeed vented in the Sheldonian that November afternoon. The assembly had been called by the Society for the Protection of Ancient Buildings (SPAB) to protest against imminent restoration and rebuilding to the west front of St Mark's Cathedral, Venice. From the Society's standpoint, such work could only amount to the destruction of the artistic and architectural treasures of St Mark's. SPAB had been formed by William Morris in March 1877 and had so far waged some lively polemical campaigns against the restorers in defence of British buildings. The defence of St Mark's which it was now undertaking represented a quantum leap forward in its activities; this was its first significant foray into the international arena and, as the campaign gathered momentum, was the first time it had registered on the national consciousness in a major way. The Oxford meeting on 15 November 1879 was not the only such occasion it had organised, but it was surely the most prestigious. Six notable speakers had been assembled to celebrate the glories of St Mark's, expound the threats they were now under, and recommend protesting to the Italian Minister of Public Works. One of these six speakers was William Morris, for whom this was the first occasion at which he spoke at his old university in a public capacity.

In his address to the first annual general meeting of SPAB in June 1878 Morris had noted that it would be crucial for the Society to spread its campaign to the rest of Europe, 'in many parts of which there has both been more to destroy and more ignorant and reckless destruction than in England' (*AWS*, I, 113). Resources were desperately lacking for such an extension of the Society's work, yet it did keep a watching brief on certain European buildings: for example, in December 1878 Morris was making efforts to get a report on St Mark's by the Frenchman Charles Yriate into the English press (*CL*, I, 502).

As secretary of SPAB, Morris had learnt in October 1879 that major works were proposed on the west front of St Mark's, and in a letter to the *Daily News*, written on 31 October and published on 1 November, he went public on the issue, warning 'what a disaster is threatened hereby to art and culture in general' (*CL*, I, 528). On Thursday 6 November a crowded meeting of the SPAB committee at its London headquarters, chaired by Percy Wyndham MP, planned a campaign involving meetings in Cambridge, Birmingham and Oxford. Henry Wallis wrote to *The Times* on the issue on 8 November, and five days later, on Thursday 13 November, a major public meeting in defence of St Mark's was held in Birmingham. The venue was the theatre of the Birmingham and Midlands Institute; the mayor of the city, Richard Chamberlain, was in the chair, and the chief speaker was William Morris, who was seconded by Samuel Timmins, a well-known local educationalist.

It is worth asking why Birmingham seemed the appropriate location for this meeting. Timmins himself noted the apparent irony of discussing the fate of St Mark's in Birmingham, 'a town so practical that it was supposed to have no taste for art' (*The Architect*, 22 November 1879, 299). Perhaps SPAB's rationale was to demonstrate to the Italian authorities that industrial England, as well as bastions of traditional culture like Oxford and Cambridge, was passionately concerned about St Mark's, and thus to dramatise the extraordinary universality of the appeal of the building and its artworks. Presumably a sequence of meetings seemed more effective, from an activist viewpoint, than a single giant one, however prestigious; in this way, one could keep the issue before the public eye for longer and build a sense of momentum and gathering strength in the campaign. More pragmatically, Morris already at this early stage of his lecturing career had a number of contacts in Birmingham. He was President of the Birmingham School of Art and had lectured on 'The Art of the People' to the Birmingham Society of Arts and the Birmingham School of Design at the latter's prize-giving ceremony in February 1879. He thus had a network of relevant contacts which may have allowed him to put a Birmingham meeting in place at relatively short notice. He may also, as a still relatively inexperienced public speaker, have wanted a warm-up before the gathering at the Sheldonian Theatre later that week. And finally, as the figure who was putting most time and effort into the St Mark's campaign, he may have wanted an event at which he would have the floor more or less to himself and be the star of the show, rather than being merely one of six distinguished speakers, as he would at Oxford two days later. We do not have to choose between these assorted speculations as to why Birmingham was chosen; all of them may have played their part, in different proportions and at more or less conscious levels.

So far as we can judge from contemporary press accounts, Morris delivered an effective speech to his Birmingham audience, building confidently upon his address in the city earlier that year. He stands before his audience as the official representative of SPAB and, as he reads out the Society's Memorial and then comments upon it, he quickly establishes an impressive historical authority:

> the church was, undoubtedly, in very good condition, and it was practically unchanged from the time of Gentile Bellini, which was about 1480. At the time he painted his picture of the church the whole of the front was entirely covered with mosaics in character with the rest of the building. Some of them, though not all, were old Greek mosaics; some of them were the later Italian mosaics, and specimens of these were still left in the church by the north transept. However, this was all altered, he [Morris] was sorry to say, in the seventeenth century. One was bound to say this, although no less a man than Titian was concerned in the alteration of the mosaics ... That was practically the last desecration that the west front suffered till some fifteen years ago, when the tide of restoration set in. (*The Architect*, 22 November 1879, 299)

With his easy command of the narrative of St Mark's development, Morris tells a compelling and comprehensive story, and the various annotations of 'laughter' and 'applause' in the *Birmingham Daily Post* account suggest that he swiftly won over his audience (14 November 1879, 5).

Morris presents himself in this speech as the omnicompetent SPAB functionary, pulling in expert testimony where appropriate, as when he evokes the architect G.E. Street's opinion that the wave in the St Mark's pavement was artistically intentional, not a structural defect that needed ironing out and restoring away. On the occasions where the speech offers aesthetic judgements that are not grounded either in historical narrative or in expert witness, as with the claims that refurbishments to the north side of the building have made it look 'inharmonious and uncomfortable' or that restoration of the south side had left it looking 'like a glittering white toy' (*The Architect*, 299), one feels that Morris probably adduced his own 1878 visit to Venice as authority for such assessments, as he would do in the Sheldonian two days later. Though his Italian trip had been so plagued by gout that he looked forward to Venice and its gondolas as the 'hobbler's Paradise', St Mark's does later feature in the list of buildings that moved him most profoundly on the expedition (*CL*, I, 483). But the brief press reports of the speech do not include such a personal reference, and even if Morris did not invoke his first-hand experience here, such fleeting aesthetic assertions are carried by the overall historical sweep and confidence of his performance.

Two days later Morris was at the Sheldonian Theatre in Oxford. We do not have any record of his private feelings at being back in his old university in a public capacity for the first time; perhaps he was simply so busy with the day's practical business that he did not have time for any. As the building filled up in the early afternoon of 15 November, he must surely have felt satisfied with the turnout, in terms of both quantity and quality. This audience of the great and the good was clearly well-disposed to the cause; what now mattered was to inform them more fully and in the process make their Artistic Indignation more resolute, so that it would stay firmly behind SPAB in what might after all prove a long and tough campaign.

But before the issue of St Mark's itself could be addressed, it appears that some ethical ground-clearing needed to be done. According to *The Architect* Morris himself posed the crucial question in his own contribution – 'But it might be asked on what grounds could Englishmen interfere' (298) – and the chairmen of both the Birmingham and Oxford meetings felt obliged to address this issue in their opening remarks. For both of them, England has a privileged role to play in any international campaign against restoration: it was caught up early in restoration mania, had done grave damage to its own ancient monuments in the grip of that obsession, but now, appropriately chastened and repentant, it could offer the lessons of its own painful recent architectural history to any nation which had not yet embarked upon this self-destructive course. A second justification for polemical interference, offered by

Dean Liddell at Oxford, involved England's long-standing literary and aesthetic relationship to Venice itself, all the way from *The Merchant of Venice* onwards. Liddell quotes several lines on the city from Byron's *Childe Harold* and concludes: 'in the name of English literature and art, in the name of Shakespeare, Otway, and Byron, by the glowing canvass of Turner, and the no less glowing pages of one whose name in this place was a household word – John Ruskin – (applause) – he asked them to plead with the Italians in the name of the hallowed front of St Mark' (*OCUJ*, 20 November 1879, 115). The long English aesthetic meditation on Venice thus gives depth and seriousness to the cultural polemics of the present, proving that contemporary 'interference' in its architectural affairs is not simply British imperial high-handedness but rather the ripe fruits of a centuries-long respect for the city.

A third line of argument justifying the right of England to pronounce on this topic concerns not Venice in general but St Mark's in particular. Mayor Chamberlain enunciates the principle rather flatly, affirming that 'St. Mark's belonged not to Venice only, but to the whole world' (*The Architect*, 299). Morris develops the point more eloquently in his two contributions. St Mark's was, he argued in his Birmingham address, 'a church made up of many different ideas' (299) or, as he elaborated at Oxford: 'No one people was represented in connection with St. Mark's: the Roman, the Greek, the Persian, the Armenian, the Arab, and the Goth, every one of these peoples was represented in that front of St. Mark's' (*JOJ*, 22 November 1879, 7). To interfere in the fate of any other Venetian building might indeed, on this showing, be impudent, but St Mark's is no ordinary church; it is, rather, a universal building, an architectural and historical encyclopaedia whose well-being appropriately concerns cultivated people well beyond its own narrow national boundaries.

The right to intervene having been thus established by the chairmen, the speakers at both meetings could then develop their polemical case in more detail. The first speaker in the Sheldonian, G.E. Street, functions as an expert architectural witness who testifies from recent personal experience that the west front of St Mark's is structurally sound. It was crucial to get this point authoritatively established right from the start in order to cut the ground from under the feet of the restorers and rebuilders (though even if structural unsoundness could have been proved, SPAB would presumably have recommended shoring-up by engineers rather than wholesale rebuilding). In an impressive *coup de théâtre*, Street at one point in his speech brandished his own personal piece of St Mark's mosaic – 'large fragments', according to the *Cambridge Review* (91) – which he had purchased from the sacristan for a few lire just before it was carted off into a canal; there could hardly have been a more effective way of dramatising how cavalierly the Italians were treating their national treasures. He defined the beauty of St Mark's as residing not in its architectural charm or in scale but in 'beauty of colour' (*OCUJ*, 115), thereby affording an opening to the second speaker, Edward Burne-Jones, who gives his testimony against restoration as a painter rather than as an architect. Burne-Jones's brief speech was the first and last he ever made in public, and presumably only Morris could have prevailed upon him to take to the podium in the first place; but how effective his intervention was in the crowded Sheldonian that November afternoon is open to doubt since, as the *Cambridge Review* noted, he read his speech 'at such a pace and in such low tones that it was difficult to catch what he said' (90).

Inaudible he may have been, but at least Burne-Jones was present on this occasion – unlike John Ruskin, who was represented *in absentia* by his long-term friend Professor Henry Acland. I have already noted Liddell's invocation of Ruskin in his opening remarks, and the latter's centrality to such a gathering as this can hardly be overstated. It was Ruskin's *Seven Lamps of Architecture* (1849) that had provided the theoretical underpinnings of the SPAB case against restoration in the first place, as acknowledged by Morris himself when he wrote to Ruskin on behalf of the Society in July 1877 asking permission to quote a famous passage from the book in its publications. And it was Ruskin more than anyone else who had given Venice its centrality in the Victorian middle-class cultural imagination with his *The Stones of Venice* (1851–53). The St Mark's campaign could accordingly be described, to adapt a phrase of Morris's in an 1880 letter to Ruskin, as 'a cause which you yourself made a cause' (*CL*, I, 569).

Not only was Ruskin not present in the Sheldonian, but his manner of refusal, as relayed by Acland, was startlingly terse: 'I am not coming, I have nothing to say' (*OCUJ*, 115). Acland did the best he could under the circumstances, reading out an eloquent passage from Ruskin's *St Mark's Rest* in praise of the threatened mosaic and then moving on, as instructed by Ruskin, to read from a letter which the latter had written to Count Alvise Zorsi, who had campaigned against an earlier phase of restoration to St Mark's in 1877. Having just restored the southern facade (on which several of the Sheldonian speakers comment very adversely), the Italian architect G.B. Meduna was in that year turning his attentions to the west face of the cathedral. To fight off such developments, Zorsi published his *Observations on the Internal and External Restorations of the Basilica of St. Mark*, to which Ruskin's letter served as a preface. So Ruskin's impassioned words – his declaration that he was 'a fosterchild of Venice; she has taught me all that I have rightly learned of the arts that are my joy' (*OCUJ*, 115) – were apt enough to the 1879 Oxford event, but they were words of the past rather than of the present; and the admirable role he had played in the earlier battle only made his absence from the Sheldonian the more striking.

In fact, by 1879, as Acland knew better than anyone else in the Theatre, Ruskin's life and career were in deep crisis. Early in 1878 he had suffered a catastrophic mental breakdown at Brantwood in the Lake District, being found naked and deranged on the morning of 23 February and remaining insane for about a month afterwards; Acland, as both personal friend and medical man, was one of the very first people notified by telegram about the crisis and travelled up to Brantwood at the first opportunity (Hilton, 669). Professional humiliation followed personal disaster when the jury's decision went against Ruskin in the court case for libel brought against him by the American expatriate artist James Abbot McNeill Whistler later that year. Reviewing Whistler's works at the Grosvenor Gallery in *Fors Clavigera*, Ruskin had famously denounced him for his 'cockney impudence' and for asking two hundred guineas for 'flinging a pot of paint in the public's face' (Cook and Wedderburn, XXIX, 160). Neither figure emerged unscathed from the trial: the judgement went against Ruskin, who had not been well enough to attend court, but Whistler was awarded derisory damages of one farthing and was bankrupted by the costs. Ruskin regarded the loss of the case as undermining his Slade Professorship at Oxford, which he accordingly resigned, writing to Liddell in November 1878:

Although my health has been lately much broken, I hesitated in giving
in my resignation of my Art-Professorship in the hope that I might still
in some imperfect way have been useful at Oxford. But the result of the
Whistler trial leaves me no further option. I cannot hold a Chair from
which I have no power of expressing judgement without being taxed for
it by British Law. (Cook and Wedderburn, XXIX, xxv)

In the wider context, moreover, Ruskin's authority as arbiter of artistic
taste had been severely damaged by the Whistler case, which demonstrated how thoroughly out of touch he now was with the most avant-
garde aspects of Victorian art.

Ruskin had thus lost his sanity (albeit temporarily), his prestigious
public post and a good measure of his general cultural authority in
1878. He had recovered enough by the following year to take certain
limited measures in defence of St Mark's. He wrote a brief *Circular
respecting Memorial Studies of St. Mark's* and contributed a set of notes to
an exhibition of ten photographs, mostly of St Mark's, which was shown
at the Society of Painters in Water Colours. He appealed for funds, both
through his own *Circular* and through the Ruskin Society of Manchester,
to commission as much copying of the threatened features of the building as he could organise, 'such casts, and colourings, and measurings,
as may be of use in time to come' (Cook and Wedderburn, XXIV, 423).
What is striking here is the difference in tone between Ruskin's efforts
on behalf of St Mark's and the SPAB campaign itself. Whereas the latter
was determined and even aggressive (to the point, indeed, of thoroughly
offending the Italian authorities), Ruskin's contributions were a despair-
ing rearguard action. Unlike SPAB, he had no hope of actually stopping
the rebuilding of the west front; the only gain he could conceive through
campaigning activity was to achieve better records for posterity of what
now, in his view, was inevitably lost.

Such efforts were of course helpful, even admirable, given the depth
of the personal crisis from which Ruskin had to rouse himself to make
them; but nothing would have more thoroughly energised the St Mark's
campaign than his presence and eloquence in the Sheldonian Theatre
on 15 November 1879. The building itself painfully underlined the fact
of his absence on this occasion. For it had been the scene of one of his
greatest triumphs on his installation as Slade Professor in February

1870. The University Museum lecture theatre had been crowded out and an alternative venue had to be found. Tim Hilton vividly evokes the scene: 'Henry Acland had the solution. He announced that the lecture would now be held in the Sheldonian Theatre. There was then a procession. It was informal, but a procession none the less. Ruskin and Acland, followed by hundreds of dons and undergraduates, walked from the University Museum, which both men had helped to found, to the Sheldonian Theatre ... There, Ruskin spoke to a rapt audience' (Hilton, 457). There is accordingly a threefold dimension to Ruskin's physical absence from the Sheldonian nine years later. He lets down a cause which he has made a cause – anti-restoration – in relation to an object – St Mark's, Venice – which he above all has called attention to, in a place – Oxford – which during his years as Slade Professor he had effectively made his own.

John Ruskin, we might say, suffers the same fate in the Sheldonian Theatre in November 1879 as William Guest suffers in Kelmscott Church at the end of Morris's *News from Nowhere*: he fades painfully away into nothingness on the threshold of the building while a lively, impassioned gathering, to which he might well have expected to be central, goes on inside without him. But if Ruskin thus fades from the scene, who steps forward to take his place? Who, in the Sheldonian, might have played the role of Dick Hammond in *News from Nowhere*, who steps forward into Kelmscott Church with an 'air of proprietorship' just as Guest vanishes from its threshold (*CW*, XVI, 209)? With the benefit of historical hindsight we can of course see that Morris is the emergent figure here, yet I suspect that this was by no means so evident to his Oxford audience. To those in a position to know, it would have been clear that Morris was putting a tremendous amount of energy as an activist into the St Mark's campaign, but whether he yet had the intellectual and cultural authority, or the personal audacity, to emerge as Ruskin's successor was another matter entirely.

Of Morris's activist credentials in the cause there could be absolutely no doubt. He it was, after all, whose letter to *The Athenaeum* in March 1877 protesting at George Gilbert Scott's restoration of Tewkesbury Minster had kicked off the whole SPAB project in the first place. The first meeting of what was to become the Society for the Protection of

Ancient Buildings took place in Morris and Co.'s premises in Queen Square on 22 March; Morris was voted honorary secretary and treasurer, drafted a manifesto over the next few days, and was the most prominent spokesperson for the organisation in the press thereafter. He had been no less dynamic in the St Mark's campaign, as I have already noted. From his letter to the *Daily News* of 1 November 1879 onwards he had been, in J.W. Mackail's fine phrase, the 'soul of the movement of protest' (Mackail, II, 5). Moreover, as we have already seen, Morris took a very prominent role at the Birmingham meeting on 13 November, discoursing learnedly on the earlier phases of restoration that St Mark's had suffered, and being rather limply succeeded by his seconder, Samuel Timmins.

But at the Oxford event two days later Morris's role was much more modest. He was now one of six speakers, and even then he was merely seconding rather than actually proposing one of the three resolutions passed. So though to every Oxford man in the room Ruskin's absence must have been eloquent enough, Morris did not, simply in terms of the structure of the occasion, dominate the meeting as an obvious successor. Indeed, if anybody in the Sheldonian that day appeared to be taking up the Ruskinian mantle, it was probably William Blake Richmond, who had taken over Ruskin's vacated Slade Professorship in 1879 and who made a long and in my view effective speech in the Sheldonian proposing the third resolution in favour of addressing a remonstrance to the Italian government (seconded by Professor Holland).

Nor is it clear, given his relatively subaltern role in the structure of the event, how successfully Morris used the limited time and opportunity he was afforded here. He was still in the relatively early days of his career as a public speaker, which had got under way with his lecture on 'The Decorative Arts' to the Trades Guild of Learning in April 1877, and just how effective he was as a performer on the podium in these early years remains open to question. The *Cambridge Review* certainly had reservations about his delivery in the Sheldonian, complaining that 'for a poet, his style is singularly unpolished, and his manner somewhat colloquial' (91). From our own contemporary standpoint, unpolished colloquialism sounds like a desirable attribute in a public speaker, and it was certainly a quality that Morris cultivated in his socialist lectures to working-class audiences in the 1880s. But the *Cambridge Review* may well be right in its implication that, in as august a gathering of the great and the good as that assembled in the Sheldonian Theatre, a more measured and elevated tone on Morris's part might have been prudent. It was certainly the case more generally that his energy and bluntness threatened to prove counterproductive in the St Marks's campaign by considerably alienating the Italian authorities (Sharp, 1993, 10–11).

But it was not only his mode of delivery that may have partly hamstrung William Morris in the Sheldonian; there is also an issue of the authority with which he speaks at this meeting. This was much less of a problem for him at the Birmingham event where the cultural stakes are, as it were, much lower. In a city 'so practical that it was supposed to have no taste for art', Morris's easy command of the history of St Mark's, his confident appeal when appropriate to expert witness, and his firm aesthetic judgements make him an entirely adequate figure on the podium. In Oxford, however, the 'standards of proof' required are a good deal higher. Throughout his St Mark's campaigning Morris appeals to the 'large body of cultivated men' that he believes will be concerned by the issue (*CL*, I, 529); and in the Sheldonian Theatre, crowded as it was with Wardens, Rectors, Principals, Provosts and Professors, he was encountering that body in its purest form. Each speaker accordingly has to establish his credentials. A recent personal visit to Venice is a beginning, but nowhere near enough; there also has to be relevant professional expertise which grounds one's judgements of the aesthetic value, architectural history and current condition of St Mark's. Ruskin's own authority, had he been present, would have rested on the massive achievement of the three volumes of *The Stones of Venice*. G.E. Street, as the first speaker, has his own position as leading architect of the Gothic Revival behind him and, as I have noted, he dramatically pressed home his eloquence by brandishing actual pieces of St Mark's before the audience. Burne-Jones and Richmond speak as well-known painters, shifting the debate away from architectural structure to aspects of St Mark's within their own professional domain, such as the beauty of the mosaics or the weathered colouring of the marble. Acland is more of a ventriloquist than a presence in his own right, being authorised to play this modest role both by his long friendship with Ruskin and by the latter's recent communication to him.

Morris's own contribution to the Sheldonian debate is, however, curiously modest, in contrast to both his Birmingham speech and to the other Oxford speakers; it is as if he has not fully decided what role he should adopt and he certainly does not emerge as a forceful intellectual presence in his own right. *Jackson's Oxford Journal* gives the most detailed report of Morris's contribution, which opens as follows:

> Mr. Morris seconded the resolution, and said he was at St. Mark's in April and May, 1878, and at that time the hoarding on the south side was taken away, and the result was as might have been expected. It looked like a piece of new sugar in the sun, colourless and blank, with scattered pieces of mosaic stuck about, and a good many of the capitals re-cut. The wood mosaics brought to his mind the gist of the whole matter. The worst that could be done to the Church was what certainly would be done, unless the intention was changed by something like the pressure of external opinion. (*JOJ*, 22 November 1879, 7)

The 'piece of new sugar' simile is presumably one of those unpolished colloquialisms which the *Cambridge Review* deplored, and to open with the personal anecdote rather than a declaration of relevant professional expertise is already perhaps a sign of weakness here. For Morris is, of course, neither architect nor painter, despite his brief efforts in both directions in earlier years. He had in fact been articled to Street in January 1856, abandoning the profession at the end of that year, so he can hardly pronounce loftily on architecture, as he did earlier at Birmingham, with his former master now sitting beside him on the platform and distinguished architects like William Burges in the audience. Nor, despite his Rossetti-inspired phase as a would-be painter in the late 1850s, can Morris possibly compete in that field with Burne-Jones and Richmond, so that art references which he confidently wielded in his Birmingham talk – the Bellini painting of St Mark's, for example – are here magicked away from him and appear in their discourse instead (Richmond's in this case). Neither does Morris invoke, as one might have expected, his own expertise as designer and craftsman to argue (as he so often does elsewhere) that contemporary craft skills are in no way the equivalent of medieval craft skills and that even with the best will in the world they cannot possibly duplicate the earlier work; it is, oddly enough, Burne-Jones at the Oxford meeting who presses home this quintessentially Morrisian point.

In contrast to the other speakers, then, Morris does not have an immediately relevant professional expertise to offer, and he therefore of necessity speaks mostly as a SPAB activist, keeping firmly before his audience's eyes the necessity of external pressure upon the Italian authorities and seeking to sharpen the polemical edge of that pressure rather more than his fellow speakers are inclined to allow; it should be, he maintains, 'polite ... but not mealy-mouthed' (*JOJ*, 7). But this is a relatively subaltern role to play in the Sheldonian meeting and certainly, in contrast with the Birmingham event two days earlier, a significant step backwards in terms of Morris's own public profile. So that although Ruskin himself is absent from Oxford on 15 November and decisively faltering on both the personal and the professional fronts, and although Morris had in so many practical ways taken up his mantle in relation to both the anti-restoration issue in general and to Venice in particular, he does not fully enforce this position in the meeting itself. His language may have been more colourful than that of some other contributors (so to that degree, I suppose, he has enforced his own cultural authority as poet), but he does not emerge as a major intellectual presence here.

It may well be that Morris's personal and intellectual debt to Ruskin inhibited him from taking the decisive step forward into the master's vacant place; and it may also be that he did not realise how overwhelming the older man's personal difficulties now were. He certainly made sustained attempts to involve Ruskin in the St Mark's campaign. He first wrote to him on 3 November 1879 urging him to send a letter to *The Times* on the subject and expressing measured optimism about the prospects of stopping the work on the west front. But no such letter was forthcoming. On 17 March 1880 Morris attended Ruskin's lecture, 'A Caution to Snakes', at the London Institution. He wrote again to Ruskin on 26 May, inviting him to either chair or address the annual general meeting of SPAB the following month. This time he ratchets up the moral pressure on the author of *The Stones of Venice*: 'I think we deserve the encouragement your voice and presence would give us: we are again going to stir the St Marks' matter' (*CL*, I, 569). However, Ruskin turned down the invitation and the chair was taken by the altogether lesser figure of Stanley Leighton, MP. Morris finally had better luck with an indirect appeal through Burne-Jones, who was always a good deal personally closer to Ruskin than he himself was; he was able to write to Henry Wallis in August 1880 to say that Ruskin had telegraphed his acceptance of a place on the international St Mark's Committee.

The tone of Morris's letters to Ruskin is highly respectful, at moments verging on that of disciple to master, humbly continuing the struggle in 'a cause which you yourself made a cause'. There is clearly an implicit acknowledgement of Ruskin's recent illness but there seems to be also an unwillingness to accept that in important respects the older man is a spent force and that it may now be necessary to go beyond him in order to advance his own campaigns and values. It is not until Morris receives a letter from Ruskin himself the following year authorising such a move that the younger man seems liberated and, like Dick Hammond, can stride purposefully into Kelmscott Church – or Oxford polemics, in our case – while Ruskin/Guest fades into relative invisibility on the threshold. For Ruskin wrote on 27 May 1880:

> Please recollect – or hereafter know – by these presents – that I am old, ill, and liable any day to be struck crazy if I get into a passion. And therefore, while I can still lecture – if I choose – on rattlesnakes' tails, I can't on anything I care about. Nor *do* I care to say more on this matter than I have done, especially since I know that the modern mob will trample to-morrow what it spares to-day. You younger men must found a new dynasty – the old things *are* passed away. (Cook and Wedderburn, XXXVII, 315)

Ruskin here at last authorises Morris and Burne-Jones to succeed him and, as we shall see, mentor and disciple will precisely enact this succession in Morris's November 1883 Oxford lecture on 'Art under Plutocracy'.

The SPAB Memorial against the restoration of St Mark's eventually collected an impressive 2,000 signatures, including those of Gladstone and Disraeli (now Lord Beaconsfield), and was duly presented to the

Italian authorities. But even before it had been presented the proposed restoration work on the building had been cancelled by the Ministry of Public Instruction, and a committee which reported back in Italy on the issue in March 1880 moved decisively to preservationist rather than restorationist principles. Whether this climbdown was due to the SPAB campaign or was an independent decision by Italian officials is a moot point; the Society was eager to claim the former, naturally; the Italians, the latter. What this triumph (if that is indeed what it was) seems to have shown to Morris is how effective Oxford could be as a mobilising centre for SPAB's campaigns. He had concluded his speech in the Sheldonian with the claim that 'he could not doubt that an appeal from this great University, where so much had been done for art, would have some effect on the people of Venice and Italy' (*JOJ*, 7). He may have been flattering his audience or he may have genuinely believed this (or both); we cannot now tell. But on the evidence of the Sheldonian meeting Oxford clearly had a critical mass of 'cultivated men' who could be galvanised at short notice and who were sure of making a major impact in the media channels of the time. Hence it was that as Morris organised the international committee on St Mark's in mid-1880 he still wanted to pack it with Oxford men, sending out invitations to Liddell of Christ Church; Mark Pattison, Rector of Lincoln; Edward Talbot, Warden of Keble; and Professor Max Müller; as well as, for instance, the American poet James Russell Lowell. Yet, as we shall see and Morris had painfully to learn, however readily the Oxford great and good came together in defence of a major symbol of European culture like St Mark's, it would be a very different matter indeed when architectural desecration was taking place in their own backyard. So Morris's next incursion into the city, over the redevelopment of Magdalen Bridge, which involved local financial and commercial interests, would constitute a very much tougher test of whether his Oxonian audience could be mobilised effectively again.

TWO

Magdalen Bridge, 1881

One night I dreamed I stood, about evening-time, on a bridge ...
Magdalen Tower stood full in front of me ... Yes! It was Oxford.

'Oxford', *Oxford and Cambridge Magazine* (April 1856, 255)

William Morris's *News from Nowhere* is a book of bridges. As a
utopian dream-vision, it is itself a bridge between the capitalist
present and a possible socialist future – though sadly for the book's
narrator, William Guest, it is a bridge that takes two-way, rather than
one-way, traffic. And bridges prove to be a recurrent motif throughout
the text. The very first indication that Guest gets that anything extraordinary is about to happen to him concerns Hammersmith Bridge: 'as
for the ugly bridge below, he did not notice it or think of it, except
when for a moment ... it struck him that he missed the row of lights
downstream' (*CW*, XVI, 4). Is the bridge still there or not? We shall
never know, but clearly the massive empirical given-ness of Victorian
capitalism has begun to shift mysteriously, as if the epistemological in-
stability of the actual bridge here allows the metaphorical bridge which
is the text itself to come fully into being.

When Guest awakens early next morning it is Hammersmith Bridge,
again, that more than anything else signals to him the momentous transformation that has taken place. As he refreshes himself by swimming

in the Thames, 'my eyes naturally sought for the bridge, and so utterly
astonished was I by what I saw, that I forgot to strike out, and went
spluttering under water again' (6). What he sees, on a second and more
leisurely look, is a bridge to end all bridges, the very Platonic essence
of a bridge made incarnate in utopia:

> Then the bridge! I had perhaps dreamed of such a bridge, but never
> seen such an one out of an illuminated manuscript; for not even the
> Ponte Vecchio at Florence came anywhere near it. It was of stone
> arches, splendidly solid, and as graceful as they were strong; high
> enough also to let ordinary river traffic through easily. Over the
> parapet showed quaint and fanciful little buildings, which I supposed to
> be booths or shops, beset with painted and gilded vanes and spirelets
> … In short, to me a wonder of a bridge. (8)

Dick Hammond at once reminds us, however, that such a utopian bridge
did not come into being all at once. *News from Nowhere* alerts us in its
very opening paragraph that there will be two phases in the building
of socialism – the immediate Morrow of the Revolution and then, a
good deal later, the fully developed new society – and there have also,
appropriately enough, been two phases in the reconstruction of Hammersmith Bridge. Sir Joseph Bazalgette's 1887 bridge first gives way to
a 'rather plain timber bridge', and only in 2003 is the glorious edifice
that Guest sees 'built, or at least opened'. There is also a 'pretty bridge'
on the rescued creek at the start of chapter IV (23), and if this is the
spirit in which all London's bridges have been refashioned in the years
after *Nowhere*'s revolution, then the capital might well now be dubbed a
'City of the Bridges', to borrow an evocative phrase from Morris's *The
Water of the Wondrous Isles* (*CW*, XX, 244).

An astonishing bridge thus serves as the first great marker of socialist
utopia, and bridges continue to have a significant presence in the text
thereafter. As he travels up the Thames with Dick and Clara, Guest
notes with relish that 'my old enemies the "Gothic" cast-iron bridges
had been replaced by handsome oak and stone ones' (XVI, 160). Bridges
serve again as vivid markers of transition when Ellen's boat comes
thrusting vigorously through the low arches of Wallingford Bridge; this
is the moment when she decisively breaks out of her confinement at

Runnymede and embarks on the new, extraordinary relationship with Guest that so dominates the later chapters of the book. And Ellen, who is herself the most crucial 'bridge' between utopia's present as we witness it in *News from Nowhere* and whatever its subsequent future may be, clearly shares Guest's passion for the Thames bridges: ' "Look!" she said, springing up suddenly from her place without any obvious effort, and balancing herself with exquisite grace and ease; "look at the beautiful old bridge ahead!" ' (189).

Bridges so far have been associated with the sensuousness and athleticism that are such attractive features of utopian life in Nowhere: with early morning swimming, with rowing on the Thames, or with Ellen's own remarkable energies. But they also preoccupy the most sedentary character in the book, the utopian expositor Old Hammond, who has lived so long in the British Museum that he has almost become one of its artefacts in his own right. For it is surely no accident that when, in the chapter 'How Matters are Managed', Hammond casts around for an example of how administrative decisions are made in a classless society he should settle on the case of 'a stone bridge substituted for some ugly old iron one, – there you have undoing and doing in one'. He proceeds to give a detailed account of how disagreements over the issue would be fought out in the neighbourhood Mote over its next few sessions, with 'arguments *pro* and *con* ... flying about, and some get printed' (88). The procedures show us an exemplary local government at work and were presumably followed in the various phases of the post-revolutionary reconstruction of Hammersmith Bridge itself. Guest is certainly impressed – 'there is something in all this very like democracy', he murmurs – and the effect of Hammond's meticulous account is to 'de-reify' the bridges of the new society. For bridges, we now come to realise, are not self-contained architectural artefacts but rather social *processes*, both in the initial debates about their construction and in their role of facilitating the movement of human traffic, in both city and countryside.

In an interview on anarchism with the Social Democratic Federation journal *Justice* in 1894, Morris at one point proposes to his interlocutor: 'Take an illustration which I have frequently used, the question of building a bridge' (Pinkney, 86). Why, then, did he so frequently use this example, as opposed, say, to the other possibilities that Old Hammond had floated but dismissed in 'How Matters are Managed' – building a town hall or clearing some inconvenient houses? The answer, I suggest, is because Morris himself, in late 1881, had been passionately caught up in debates about (re)building a bridge. For on Thursday 27 October of that year, in the hall of University College, he made his second public speech in Oxford at a meeting held to protest against the plans of the Local Board to rebuild and widen Magdalen Bridge. Oxford had been only a forum for Morris and SPAB in 1879 during the St Mark's campaign; its value was as a communications centre, where the great and the good could be speedily assembled in ways that would make the maximum impact in the national and international press. Now, however, the same enemy, architectural philistinism, threatened the very fabric of Morris's beloved city rather than some distant European cultural monument. The issues suddenly came much closer to home, with a much sharper politics to them; and, as the reverberations of this matter in *News from Nowhere* and elsewhere a decade later suggest, the scars of the Magdalen Bridge campaign were profound indeed.

It is clear, at any rate, that Morris's personal feelings about Magdalen Bridge ran as deep as those of William Guest for the various bridges he encounters on the Thames above and below Oxford. In his reminiscences of Morris, Arthur Stringer gives us a memorable vignette, though we cannot date it: 'I can remember, too, one bright morning on the High, in Oxford, as he walked with his short, quick, stocky steps out across Magdalen Bridge, and let his eyes wander musingly along the waters of the Cherwell. He suddenly drew in a great breath of air, scented with the smell of flowers from the Botanical Gardens, and gasped out: "My eyes, how good it all is!"' (Stringer, 128).

Indeed, Magdalen Bridge seems to have been not just a beautiful but a positively utopian place to Morris and his undergraduate set in the 1850s; for it is on the Bridge, looking up to the Tower, that the anonymous author of 'Oxford' in the *Oxford and Cambridge Magazine* for April 1856 finds himself at the end of that article. This well-researched piece, which ranges widely across the history of the university from the Middle Ages as well as being alert to the University Commissions of 1850 and 1852, trenchantly criticises the religious, intellectual, social and sexual narrowness of official University life. But it also has some very lively evocations of the ways that undergraduates unofficially educate each other and it concludes with a utopian dream vision, which first comes to the narrator as he stands on Magdalen Bridge, of a transfigured Oxford open to all classes and to all modern intellectual currents. I need hardly underline how proleptic this narrative device is of Morris's later literary works, and to have such a hallowed bridge threatened by unsympathetic rebuilding might well prompt one into the most determined of defensive campaigns.

From mid-century on the pace of building and rebuilding in Victorian Oxford had accelerated dramatically. In his biography of Morris J.W. Mackail dates this epoch from George Gilbert Scott's new Broad Street front to Exeter College, which replaced what Burne-Jones termed the 'tumbly old buildings' in which he and Morris had spent some of their time as students; it was this piece of modernisation, between 1854 and 1856, which 'opened the disastrous era of rebuilding among the Oxford colleges' (Mackail, I, 51). Peter Howell, in his fine study of Oxford architecture in the *History of the University of Oxford*, pushes Mackail's date on just a fraction: 'During the 1860s the amount of building activity going on in the University was tremendous, and the pace that was now set was to be kept up until the First World War' (*HUO*, VII, 2, 741).

We find slight rumblings of discontent about developments at Oxford in Morris's correspondence in the months after the St Mark's meeting. In August 1880 he wrote to a correspondent in Salisbury about unwelcome developments in that city: 'I remember both the Bridge & the buildings by St. Thomas' well: they are just the sort of buildings whose destruction is desolating so many of our English towns, and of which the ordinary, what I should call "Academical" Archeologist takes no notice. Oxford is a most miserable example of this' (*CL*, I, 587).

But early in 1881 a threat to Oxford emerged which galvanised Morris and SPAB into action rather than vague grumbling. The Society got wind of a scheme to widen Magdalen Bridge by twenty feet in order to allow trams to pass across it, having been tipped off by its Oxford members and having spotted a newspaper article on the newly formed City of Oxford and District Tramways Company (a copy of the latter exists in the SPAB archives, with a note by Morris on its back saying 'to be attended to'). The defence of the bridge was something of a departure for the Society, which had hitherto tended to concentrate on medieval buildings under threat. Magdalen Bridge, by contrast, was an elegant classical structure, designed by John Gwynn as Surveyor to the Oxford Paving Commissioners and built by John Randall. Work had begun on it in 1772 and the Bridge was completed ten years later. Significantly, in view of the debates around its widening in 1881, Gwynn's bridge had itself replaced an earlier structure in order to facilitate traffic flow on the main route from London to Oxford (Venning, 25).

Chris Miele has sketched the internal disputes within SPAB in January 1881 over how to proceed in the Magdalen Bridge affair, with the backwoodsmen of the general committee suddenly turning up at the Society's Buckingham Street headquarters to vote down the polemical recommendations of the smaller, hard-core restoration committee. Hence it was, in Miele's words, that SPAB 'was forced to tread a little more carefully than Morris, left to his own devices, would have wished' (Hunter, 35). It was perhaps on account of these internal wrangles that the Society's secretary, Newman Marks, wrote tentatively to Morris's Oxford friend Charles Faulkner on 26 January asking him 'to whom we could apply, & how we could best move in this matter' (SPAB 1, 26 January 1881).

Whether as a result of a prompt reply from Faulkner or not, Marks on 31 January sent a protest letter on behalf of SPAB to the mayor and Corporation of Oxford. Two distinct arguments are opened by this document. On the one hand, the scheme to widen the bridge is presented as the brutal intrusion of philistine commercial interests into the immemorial aesthetic harmony of Oxford's built and natural environment. On the other hand, the impulse to widen may be due to factors more acceptable than the depradations of 'a mercantile company'. For it is quite possible, Marks concedes, 'that the necessities of the increasing population of the neighbourhood may make it expedient to increase the facility of traffic', but in this case, he believes, such necessities can be satisfied while leaving the bridge in effect intact.

On 22 February, having had no reply to his letter to the mayor, Marks wrote to Faulkner asking him for advice on publishing the letter and requesting him to meet and if possible influence a fellow academic who was serving as one of the directors of the new tramway company.

In the event SPAB did go public, reprinting its letter to the mayor in *The Times* for 12 April and eliciting a remarkable response from John Brunton, the engineer of the tramway company. Brunton wrote to the Society in order to repudiate 'the impression that the Tramway Company had anything to do with the suggestion for widening the Bridge, such widening not being necessary to their accommodation' (SPAB 1, 13 April 1881). As we might expect, Marks was jubilant about this unexpected concession, declaring cheerfully to Brunton in his reply that the latter's admission 'will make our task easier in opposing the scheme' (14 April 1881). He was to be proved wrong, but Brunton's contribution provided him with useful ammunition, none the less, and Marks accordingly gave prominence to it in a second official protest letter to the chairman and members of the Oxford Local Board on 5 May.

He had in the meantime been canvassing wider support for the cause. Most respondents were sympathetic, but some of the most tried and tested warhorses of the 1879 St Mark's campaign suddenly fell at this particular hurdle. Dean Liddell wrote from Christ Church that 'No one can be more strongly opposed both to the widening of Magd. Bridge & to the Tramway-system in Oxford than I am. But I am powerless' (22 June 1881). Such apathy on the part of official Oxford later prompted its Professor of Poetry, J.C. Shairp, to lament to Newman Marks that

> It is little more than a year ago since I attended a large and influential meeting of members of the University convened in the Sheldonian Theatre, and presided over by the Dean of Christ Church, to lift up the voice of cultivated England against the changes about to be made in St. Marks, Venice. The meeting [was] in every way worthy of Oxford, and the speeches made by the Dean and others were powerful appeals to the love of the beautiful & venerable in architecture & art. How is it that this enthusiasm so entirely slumbers, while a far worse and more uncalled for desecration is going on under our own eyes? (14 December 1881)

It was no doubt a similar feeling of frustration that prompted Morris himself to take up the cudgels on behalf of the bridge on 16 July as he drafted a letter to the *Pall Mall Gazette* on 'the threatened destruction of Magdalen Bridge, which it is much to be feared is imminent' (*CL*, II, 56).

The *Gazette* did not in the event publish the letter, which none the
less gives an eloquent statement of what Morris takes to be architecturally and aesthetically at stake:

> Magdalen Bridge has a value quite apart from its own considerable
> architectural excellence, a value which it is hard to exaggerate: for it
> forms an essential part of a group of buildings quite unrivalled of its
> kind in the United Kingdom: the splendour of the great Tower, the
> Hall & the Chapel, and the beauty of the low block of buildings which
> run along the street west from the tower, all this stately mass of correct
> and well developed mediaeval architecture is not injured but helped by
> the pleasing primness of the Botanical Gardens, and the naif classical-
> lity (not perhaps as un-Gothic as it would be) of the beautiful Bridge:
> in short it must not be forgotten that these buildings of Magdalen are
> essentially part of the street, and look almost as if they had grown
> up out of the roadway: any injury done to the street will injure them
> fatally, and the result will strike even those who have not much noticed
> the separate parts which go to make up the lovely group.
>
> Moreover Magdalen Bridge and its surroundings form the main
> entrance to Oxford, to that famous High Street, which is the heart of
> the most important town of England for mingled artistic & historical
> interest. (*CL*, II, 56)

A bridge, once again, turns out not to be a self-contained artefact. It is
more of a relational force than an entity in its own right, pulling into
a greater whole the assorted objects that surround it, whether these
be the two banks of the river that it connects or, as here, the other
buildings that surround it.

Having evoked what may be lost, Morris then turns to the arguments of the modernisers. 'The traffic across Magdalen Bridge being
usually but small', it cannot be adduced as a reason for widening the
thoroughfare – though Morris also asserts the uncompromising principle
that even if the volume of traffic were sufficient to cause 'considerable
inconvenience' on the existing bridge, that inconvenience should be put
up with for the sake of the architectural merit of the site. 'Nor can the
tramway now being laid be pleaded as a cause for the rebuilding of the
Bridge', since, in what he clearly hopes will be his letter's rhetorical
killer-punch, Morris declares that the engineer of the tramway company
has written to SPAB precisely to that effect. The widening scheme has

therefore, in Morris's view, 'only to be mentioned to be condemned by all cultivated men' (*CL*, II, 56).

It is clear already from these arguments that we are in a very different terrain from many of the high-profile cases that had absorbed Morris's energies since the formation of SPAB in March 1877. The majority of these – Tewkesbury Minster, Canterbury Cathedral, Southwell Minster, St Alban's Cathedral – had been projects of ecclesiastical restoration and had aimed to return the building to an earlier, supposedly 'purer' state of its historical being. In his public attacks on such proposals, Morris had to defeat the underlying ideology here, arguing that not only was much genuine art and history destroyed in the process but that even the 'restored' areas were just modern fabrications or (in his more polemical term) forgeries rather than any kind of liberated historical authenticity. When the driving force of rebuilding was an ideology of this kind, then the tactic of reasoned persuasion, the appeal to 'men of cultivation' to see the light and switch over to conservation rather than restoration, was a plausible way forward – even if Morris liked to season it with a good deal of vigorous abuse of the restorers too.

But Morris was also involved in campaigns where this was not the case, notably in his defence of the Wren churches in the City of London in April 1878. Here it was not a matter of restoration but of the actual demolition of buildings, and the driving force of this process ultimately lay well beyond the Church itself. In his letter to *The Times* Morris complains that 'four more churches are to be sacrificed to the Mammon-worship and want of taste of this great city', and asks angrily: 'Is it absolutely necessary that every scrap of space in the City should be devoted to money-making...?' (*CL*, I, 477–8). He develops the theme in his address to the first annual general meeting of SPAB in June of the same year: 'even now mere cynically brutal destruction, not veiling itself under any artistic pretence, is only too common: it is still only too commonly assumed that any considerations of Art must yield if they stand in the way of money interests' (*AWS*, I, 117). Such ruthless financial interests might occasionally be slowed down by the Society's campaigning, with its rational appeals to the 'men of taste'; the commercial philistines might lose a battle here and there, under the weight of such polemical pressures. But they could not be fundamentally defeated by such means, as Morris in his socialist phase just a couple of years later would clearly acknowledge. This category of campaigns would accordingly propel Morris beyond the rational persuasive discourse of SPAB altogether, towards direct class confrontation with those bourgeois forces which were sweeping away the art and architecture of the past in the name of private profit.

The Magdalen Bridge issue was a tricky case for SPAB. Local business interests certainly came into play, with a new tram company concerned to maximise profits; but there were wider social implications too. For the widening of the bridge was also a matter of local government trying to manage an expanding city and its changing patterns and technologies of mobility, or, as Morris put it emphatically in November 1881, 'the new Cowley dog-holes must needs slay Magdalen Bridge!' (*CW*, XXII, 130). In this case the relational force of the bridge extends well beyond even the group of neighbouring buildings which it organises into an aesthetic whole; it reaches out into issues of city planning, demographics, and transport pressures. Malcolm Graham in *The Suburbs of Victorian Oxford* has noted that 'the mushrooming growth of East Oxford startled few Victorian commentators, perhaps because so few really knew of its existence'. For the typical middle-class Oxonian, whose horizons were confined to the city centre and the new suburb of North Oxford, 'could easily remain unaware of the town that had developed beyond Magdalen Bridge' (Graham, 103–4). The project to widen the bridge for a tramline was thus perhaps the first time that this emergent eastern suburb had fully impinged on the ancient university centre. Its 'dog-holes' were in fact mostly homes for the thrifty artisan, priced beyond the means of the low-paid or the irregularly employed, though one or two pockets of slum development did creep into the new estates going up. And if new building and migration inwards were causing the demand for new transport links, those links in turn, as Morris never says in his 1881 campaign but must surely have realised, would cause further development and growth once they were up and running, in an accelerating spiral; and Malcolm Graham has indeed shown how quickly new speculative developments were inspired by the tramway route and terminus.

To mount a fully adequate defence of Magdalen Bridge one would have to engage with this whole complex terrain, which Morris and his allies in this particular case never did in any depth. Yet the underlying dynamic at work here – from the bridge to a group of buildings to the city as a changing whole – may well be a factor in Morris's later repeated insistence on the need to extend the meaning of the word 'art' to encompass not just formal artworks but also the totality of the external surroundings of our lives, in a concentric movement out from a painting to buildings to a neighbourhood to cities to the wider natural environment. Losing the Magdalen Bridge campaign may after all, in a curious dialectical reversal, have been a major step forward in Morris's developing thought.

Morris and SPAB had by late 1881 created enough of a stir for the national press to turn its attention to these Oxonian issues:

> The widening of Magdalen-bridge has been in contemplation for some years as a means of meeting the growing requirements of the rapidly-increasing suburbs of Oxford. The Local Board are now proposing to carry out the alterations as being rendered still more necessary by the tramway which, passing down the High-street, is carried over it. The proposal has led, somewhat late in the day, to the convening of a public meeting for its consideration. (*T*, 28 November 1881, 4)

Whereas Morris began his letter to the *Pall Mall Gazette* with an evocation of the architectural value which urban modernity threatens, *The Times* begins its report on the protest meeting in University College on 27 October 1881 with an evocation of those very forces of modernity, which rhetorically tilts its reportage in favour of the improvers, however scrupulously neutral its reporter subsequently attempts to be. But Morris certainly shared the newspaper's view of the belatedness of the protest, reflecting in December 1881 that 'if we had begun a year ago we might have saved the Bridge' (*CL*, II, 86).

The hall of University College, in which Morris was to speak again – this time on socialism – in November 1883, had been subject to what Peter Howell memorably terms the 'fashionable *furor Gothicus*' of late-eighteenth-century Oxford. As University sentiment came to feel that classical styles were out of place in Oxford, so the hall had undergone an 'ultra-Gothicization' (*HUO*, VII, 2, 730). So that, though the Magdalen Bridge meeting was presumably held in University College as a matter of convenience, through the good offices of Charles Faulkner who was a Fellow there, Morris may well have felt that the semiotics of the hall were on his side: if they powerfully signalled that classicism had no place in the University, they surely also subliminally suggested that Victorian tramways had no role there either.

To what extent the meeting emulated the exemplary democracy of Old Hammond's bridge-building Mote in *News from Nowhere* we cannot really be sure from the brief report in *The Times*. The Dean of Westminster, George Granville Bradley, was in the chair, and representatives from the Oxford Local Board as well as SPAB protestors such as Charles Kegan Paul, Richard Tyrwhitt and John Henry Middleton turned up, so there was genuine debate rather than Sheldonian-style self-satisfied unanimity in the hall. Morris made a speech along the lines of his *Pall Mall Gazette* letter, insisting that the proposed widening of the bridge by twenty feet would destroy the entrance to what he called 'the most beautiful city, with the ugliest surroundings in England'. The Reverend Henry George Woods of Trinity College, who was SPAB's local representative in Oxford, took the highly uncompromising stance which we have already seen Morris adopt in his draft letter to the *Gazette*; for Woods argued that 'it was the duty of all to submit to some inconvenience and loss of time – a minute now and then, or a wrecked carriage – rather than meddle with the bridge for utilitarian purposes' (*T*, 28 November 1881, 4). The image of the wrecked carriage here might well have seemed a *reductio ad absurdum* of the SPAB case; yet it does dovetail with the principle of sacrifice on behalf of ancient buildings which Morris had firmly enunciated in his address to the second annual general meeting of the Society in June 1879: 'I am not so anxious for the reputation of a practical man as to shrink from declaring that, in my opinion, *great* sacrifices of apparent and immediate convenience should have been made in their behalf' (*AWS*, I, 122).

The three Local Board members, Messrs Child, Harcourt and Gamlen, defended their proposals, suggesting that the beauty of the bridge might thereby be enhanced rather than diminished. The ensuing deadlock seemed as though it might be broken by the lateral thinking of a Professor Earle, who recommended the building of a second bridge to relieve the strain of traffic over the Cherwell. Earle's suggestion certainly fitted in with general SPAB policy, for in its manifesto Morris had asserted that if a building 'has become inconvenient for its present use', one should 'raise another building rather than alter or enlarge the old one' (*AWS*, I, III). A relevant example in fact came up just a few years later: Morris noted in his sixth annual report in 1883 that in the case of Chipping Ongar Church the Society was urging upon the authorities the necessity of building an additional church for an increasing population rather than simply extending the old one. But in the case of Magdalen Bridge the Society did not seem prepared to encompass any compromise with the modernisers, so Earle's suggestion of a second bridge came to nothing, and a SPAB-inspired resolution was passed by the meeting deprecating any interference with the existing bridge and setting up a committee to pursue the campaign.

The question of how best to sustain the pressure certainly occupied Morris intensely for the next month or so. On 29 October he sent Woods a draft memorial, or petition, against the Board's proposals, along with some preliminary thoughts on how to get it and its signatures into the national press. Four days later he confided privately to Woods that 'I for my part never thought there was any chance of saving the Bridge', but none the less he does not 'like to be beaten without a fight'. He also admits, again confidentially, that he does after all think that even with rebuilding a good deal of the character of the bridge can be saved, and he acknowledges that the SPAB argument has ideally to engage the new realities of the changing city, not just dig in stubbornly in defence of the architectural status quo; it would therefore be helpful to urge the Board to get a 'report on the best way of relieving the traffic from a *council of architects*' (*CL*, II, 74).

By 4 November SPAB tactics had defined themselves further. There were now to be two memorials, one conducted by Woods within Oxford itself and collecting signatures of residents against the proposed widening of the bridge, and the second aimed at a wider, national public opinion and therefore seeking signatures from 'men of weight throughout the country'. It is worth noting that the national memorial reverts to a hard line on the traffic issue, stubbornly affirming that 'the exigences of traffic do not at present necessitate the rebuilding of the Bridge (since it is already wide enough for three vehicles abreast)' (*CL*, II, 78).

By 7 December Morris was able to report to Woods that the national memorial had reached one hundred signatures, though his efforts to get both text and names into the press were proving more of a struggle than he had expected. *The Times* eventually obliged by publishing on 13 December a selection of signatories to the memorial, including L. Alma-Tadema, Robert Browning, Henry Broadhurst MP, Sir Henry Cole, J. Russell Lowell, John Ruskin, G.E. Street, Alfred Tennyson and the Duke of Westminster. Morris now wanted to press the Oxford Local Board to receive a deputation of signatories to present the memorial to them. Shrewd activist that he was, he knew that a refusal would suit his purposes better than the Board's acceptance of this apparently ingenuous proposal: 'a refusal to receive our deputation would be quite as useful to us, or more useful than their receiving it; all we want is publicity for our memorial and its names' (*CL*, II, 89). The Board did indeed refuse at its meeting on 4 January 1882, as reported by *The Times* on 16 January, and on 12 January Morris was drafting a letter to them deploring their refusal and containing the text of the national memorial with representative signatures.

The local memorial, meantime, had collected 352 signatures, including that of Morris's future biographer, J.W. Mackail. Officially signed by Philip Burne-Jones (who had come up to University College in 1880) and addressed to the chairman and members of the Oxford Local Board, it declared that 'A strong feeling has, for the last 2 years, existed in Oxford on the proposed alteration in Magdalen Bridge, connected indirectly with the laying down of Tramways, etc' (SPAB 1). W.B. Richmond, as Slade Professor of Art, went so far as to recommend direct action to his undergraduate audiences, suggesting that they should collectively march out of the lecture hall and pull up the rails of the tramway. But no matter how much pressure and publicity SPAB generated through its two-pronged attack, the Board remained adamant, and work on the bridge – the destruction of the bridge, to adopt the Society's parlance – proceeded apace.

In his letter of 3 November 1881 to Henry George Woods, Morris had announced that, although he had no hope of actually saving the bridge, he 'looked upon the affair as a good occasion for making a general stand against destruction at Oxford, because *it is a public structure*'

(*CL*, II, 74). And certainly from this time onwards Oxford was firmly in his and SPAB's campaigning sights. Morris had various allies in Oxford who would keep him and the Society abreast of threatening architectural developments. There was Woods himself, its local correspondent, living at 28 Holywell Street. Another useful contact was Ingram Bywater, Greek scholar and Fellow of Exeter College. Contacts between Morris and Bywater had begun, it seems, even before Morris's SPAB campaigns. Bywater's biographer remarks: 'After the year 1871, when William Morris acquired Kelmscott Manor, his house near Lechlade, he too was among Bywater's most welcome visitors. Though he rarely spent a night at Oxford, Morris was often to be seen in Bywater's rooms in Exeter … Dressed as he commonly was in blue serge, he looked as much like a yachtsman as a poet or artist' (W. Jackson, 41).

Six years younger than Morris, Bywater seems an unlikely friend and ally in many respects. 'His interests were severely limited', remarks William Jackson, discouragingly, and his was 'always the life of an Oxford scholar' in all respects (iv). The points of contact with Morris are largely circumstantial: Bywater, like Morris, had Welsh blood in his veins; he had been to school with William De Morgan, later a key artistic and political co-worker of Morris's; and as an undergraduate at Queen's College between 1858 and 1862 he had been influenced by Carlyle's writings. In many other respects, however, Bywater's tastes could not have been further from William Morris's. He was a very close friend of Walter Pater's during their undergraduate days and after, thereby sharing in some of the obloquy that attached to Pater in Oxford after the publication of his *Studies in the History of the Renaissance* in 1873. His special taste in English literature was for the eighteenth century, a period which Morris himself could not endure; and his most sympathetic contemporary writer was Matthew Arnold, about whose relation to Morris I shall have more to say hereafter. Insofar as he had any politics, Bywater was a Liberal and wholly out of sympathy with Morris's socialism, though he did give some support to Paris Commune refugees in Oxford and later attended at least one of Morris's socialist lectures in the city. Moreover, his close friendship with Mark Pattison, Rector of Lincoln, and their shared ideal of scientific scholarship meant that

Bywater had little sympathy for any of the contemporary educational movements that sought to broaden Oxford's influence within the nation socially and geographically.

But on issues related to the Society for the Protection of Ancient Buildings, at least, and possibly on matters of book collecting, Bywater and Morris could find common ground. Bywater was dismayed by the architectural results of the Neo-Gothic Revival in mid-century Oxford, from which Exeter College had suffered as badly as any when in 1854 Sir Gilbert Scott had persuaded its Fellows to replace seventeenth-century buildings with new architecture built in the style of the thirteenth, as fine a piece of modern 'forgery' as any Morris fulminated against in his later SPAB campaigns. Bywater was accordingly an early SPAB supporter, playing some part in the St Mark's campaign of 1879, and thereafter, in the words of his biographer, he 'occasionally gave the Secretary a hint of an intended "restoration"' (W. Jackson, 41–2). It may therefore possibly have been he who had tipped off the Society about the plans to widen Magdalen Bridge in the first place.

Another significant figure who linked the worlds of Oxford and the Society for the Protection of Ancient Buildings was James Bryce, MP, whom Morris had first come to know through the Eastern Question agitation of 1876–78 and then worked with on the National Liberal League. Bryce was a prominent member of that generation of academic Liberals who first made their mark with the *Essays on Reform* in 1867 and about whom Christopher Harvie has written illuminatingly in *The Lights of Liberalism*; he had been an undergraduate at Trinity College from 1857 to 1862, a Fellow of Oriel from 1862 and Regius Professor of Civil Law from 1870. Morris praised Bryce fulsomely as a representative of the University of Oxford in seconding a vote of thanks to him at the fifth annual meeting of the Society in June 1882, claiming that there were many others amidst the dreaming spires who shared Bryce's distaste at the architectural destruction at work there. Bryce himself had an impressive record of activism at Oxford over the years, committing himself to the abolition of religious tests, the cause of University Extension, the establishment of Toynbee Hall, and the promotion of research; and we can therefore imagine him as a strong backer of Morris's Oxford campaign within SPAB itself.

However, by the time Morris came to deliver his report to the fifth annual meeting he was publicly admitting defeat over Magdalen Bridge, which was even as he spoke being rebuilt in a way that in his view would utterly ruin the beauty of its proportions. Nor was this the only piece of architectural vandalism he had to report from Oxford that year: Beam Hall, a picturesque sixteenth-century house opposite Merton College, was under threat, and Brasenose College had sold for scrap metal the group of sculptures, copied from a seventeenth-century design of John of Bologna, from their front quadrangle. The latter piece of cultural vandalism seems spectacularly to bear out Morris's private remark that 'a don ... who thinks himself a man of business will sometimes do what no honest merchant will ever do' (Elton, 121).

Among the many discouragements met with by SPAB in its campaigns, Morris grandly declared in his report, 'none, perhaps, are more grievous than the hopelessness of attempting to prevent constant acts of stupid barbarism from being perpetrated by the University of Oxford' (Morris, 1882). It was becoming abundantly clear, then, that the disfigurement of Magdalen Bridge was not a one-off piece of architectural vandalism, but rather a particularly telling instance of a more systemic assault on Oxford's ancient fabric. If classical or medieval culture could not survive here, of all places, what chance did it have of clinging on elsewhere, and why was Oxford University, so fervent in the defence of St Mark's just a few years earlier, proving so unable or unwilling to defend its own architectural inheritance? What did it say of the relation of the University to the wider society, Morris would now be compelled to ask himself, if the former were so spinelessly unable to resist the latter's relentlessly modernising impulses?

Work on Magdalen Bridge was eventually finished in 1883, and the *Oxford Magazine* remarked, quite possibly with Morris and SPAB in mind, that 'the widening of Magdalen Bridge is now a *fait accompli*. Prophets who lifted up their voices against Philistia are doomed to a pleasant disappointment ... it must be confessed that a slight loss of beauty at the city end is more than made up for by unexpected gain at the other' – that gain supposedly consisting in a handsome entry to the city with a worthier outlook over the glory of trees and pinnacles beyond (*OM*, 24 October 1883, 319). However, not long after these complacent words were penned a new controversy broke out over whether there was to be a single or double tram line across the Bridge: the Tramway Company and the Local Board were locked in dispute, and petitions for and against the double line were being busily organised in the city and university. The new battle was clear evidence, in the view of one correspondent to the *Oxford Magazine*, that 'it was solely for the sake of the tram-cars and in no wise for that of the other traffic that this most deplorable alteration' to the bridge had been made (*OM*, 21 May 1884, 253). The horse-drawn trams, which lasted in Oxford up until the First World War, look quaint enough to us now in old photographs, but garishly decorated as they were with adverts for Van Houten's Cocoa, Nixey's Blacklead, Bryant and May's Matches and A.H. Bull Drapers, they must surely have appalled Morris, who declared in *Commonweal* in November 1889 that 'an advertisement is, in short, an act of war' (*J*, 624) and whose final public speech in January 1896 was to be delivered to the Society for Checking the Abuses of Public Advertising.

We do not have a record of Morris's own response to the completion of the rebuilding of the bridge, and clearly by late 1883 it was no longer the first thing on his mind. For on the very same page on which the *Oxford Magazine* reflects on the compensations allegedly afforded by the widened bridge, it also notes that 'the Russell Club, hitherto comparatively little known in Oxford, seems likely to struggle into some prominence this Term. It is announced that Mr. William Morris will deliver a Lecture on "Democracy and Art"' (24 October 1883, 319). One could always be sure that Oxford had a decent-sized constituency of 'cultivated men' to whom one could appeal in the case of architectural threats like those to St Mark's or Magdalen Bridge, even if they turned out in the end not to be numerous or active enough to prevent such developments, as in the latter case. Now, however, Morris was about to embark on the much more difficult task of carrying that cultivated middle-class audience with him towards revolutionary socialism, of galvanising SPAB sympathisers into becoming the militant activists of what contemporaries would soon be calling a 'new Oxford Movement'.

Morris's defeat on the Magdalen Bridge issue in 1881 gradually changes the character of Oxford in his general cultural and political writings, as we can see clearly if we trace relevant references through from the

1882 *Hopes and Fears for Art* collection. In a lecture on 'The Prospects of Architecture in Civilization', delivered in March 1881 when the bridge campaign was just getting under way, Morris offered a buoyant vision of the early growth of Oxford. In 'the times of art', he claims, urban expansion was sensitively integrated into its natural environment, and thus 'much as I know I should have loved the willowy meadows between the network of the streams of Thames and Cherwell; yet I should not have been ill content as Oxford crept northward from its early home of Oseney, and Rewley, and the Castle, as townsman's house, and scholar's hall, and the great College and the noble Church hid year by year more and more of the grass and flowers of Oxfordshire' (*CW*, XXII, 130). This benign, celebratory vision can still crop out occasionally in Morris's later work, as it does memorably in an address on 'Town and Country' which he gave in Manchester in 1894: 'My familiarity with Oxford makes it easy for me to see a mediaeval town of the more important kind: a place of some extent within its ancient walls, but the houses much broken by gardens and open spaces within the walls, and without them, a small estate it may be called, the communal property of the freemen' (Mackail, II, 303). But even back in 1881 the celebratory tone had been sharply undercut by a polemical footnote about the Magdalen Bridge issue appended to the lecture eight months after its first delivery.

In 'Architecture and History' in 1884 the utopian dimensions of Oxford still outweigh its present despoliation. In his account of the life and conditions of fourteenth-century craftsmen Morris finds himself turning to the city for his positive examples. Every free man had a share in the pasture lands of the country, and 'Port Meadow, at Oxford, for instance, was the communal pasture of the freemen of that city'. If art in those days was widespread, with skill in it being the rule and not the exception, then the clinching example that at once springs to mind is 'the tower of Merton College Chapel at Oxford ... carried out by ordinary masons, under the superintendence of the Fellows of the College'. The past–present contrast is now painfully active in the prose itself, not just appended as a footnote; and thus the 'wretched tinkering that the present Fellows have allowed to be perpetrated on their beautiful succursal house, St. Albans' Hall' shows how dismally far we have fallen from the 'times of art' (*CW*, XXII, 305–6). But it is the positive vision which still predominates, and the negative modern counter-instance which feels contingent and localised.

But elsewhere the balance shifts decisively, and it is the negative which comes increasingly to the fore. 'The History of Pattern-Designing' (1882) contains a ferocious attack on the crass materialism of the University authorities, who have 'treated the beauty of Oxford as if it were a matter of no moment, as if their commercial interests might thrust it aside without any consideration. To my mind in so doing they have disgraced themselves'. The utopian medieval vision of the city can now not be evoked directly, it has been too ravaged in the present for that. All that remains of it is a faint – though educationally crucial – shadow of its former self; for 'there are many places in England where a young man may get as good book-learning as in Oxford; not one where he can receive the education which the loveliness of the grey city used to give us' (*CW*, XXII, 232). 'Grey' from this point on becomes Morris's most characteristic epithet for Oxford (and indeed his most honorific term for medieval English buildings in general), though, as Peter Howell has pointed out, the increasing use of the yellower Clipsham stone in nineteenth-century University and city building means that for us today 'the regular description of Oxford by William Morris and others as "grey" now seems puzzling' (*HOU*, VII, 2, 749). The claim that it is the architecture rather than the academic learning that takes place within its precincts that constitutes Oxford's deepest contribution to education is a crucial one for Morris, and in it, as we shall see, the seeds of his later theoretical disagreements with Matthew Arnold already lie implicit.

By the time we get to Morris's later accounts of Oxford, such as that in 'The Influence of Building Materials upon Architecture' of 1892, the utopian medieval dimension has been lost entirely. Morris there offers a page-long screed against Oxford University, 'which is such a lamentable example of all kinds of architectural errors and mistakes, and I might almost say crimes' (*CW*, XXII, 400). The failure to secure decent stone for roof slates, and the replacement of the inadequate stone slates by cheaper and utterly inappropriate green Westmoreland slates, arouses a withering contempt for Oxonian penny-pinching. With insider's information presumably gleaned from Charles Faulkner, Morris asserts sarcastically that University College saved itself 'the enormous sum of thirty pounds, I believe, in roofing the whole with the thin slates instead of the good ones' (401). It is perhaps surprising, given Morris's topic here, that he makes no mention of Keble College, built between 1868 and 1883, and for which William Butterfield had controversially chosen brick rather than stone as his material. Brick was cheaper than stone, just as thin slates were in comparison with good ones; and to this extent Keble would precisely fit Morris's polemic here. But one could argue another case about the new college, which would see its proximity to the new suburb of North Oxford as making brick the contextually appropriate material; and this was more difficult terrain for Morris, who seems never to have fully thought through the issue of population growth in Victorian Oxford.

We can therefore see that across Morris's general evocations of Oxford in his prose writings the balance between utopian reimagining and angry polemic has shifted decisively in favour of the latter – partly, as I shall show later, because Morris's Oxonian utopianism has in the later years been siphoned off into an ambitious 're-Oxfordisation' of society in his *News from Nowhere*. The Magdalen Bridge affair had revealed a profound fissure between Morris's ideal Oxford – 'a town all of whose houses are beautiful ... Rouen or Oxford thirty years ago' (*CW*, XXIII, 148) – and the actual city and University of 1881. But before he accepted that gap as an irremediable fait accompli he would make one more sustained effort, through five visits as a socialist lecturer over a twelve-month period, to recall Oxford back to its Arnoldian 'best self' or Platonic essence. In 1890 he wrote that 'the Middle Ages, so to say, saw the promised land of Socialism from afar' (*CW*, XXII, 388); and therefore the medieval university city, with its ancient architecture still in Morris's view emitting subliminal messages about the spirit of association and the Ruskinian creative freedom of the craftsman, seemed to him a place that might yet reassert its own ideal values against the philistinism that its capitulation over Magdalen Bridge had revealed.

THREE

The Democratic Federation at Oxford, 1883–84

These are the days of combat.

William Morris, 'Art and Socialism' (*CW*, XXIII, 212)

'Combat' for Morris meant resituating his earlier campaigns, whether on behalf of the Society for the Protection of Ancient Buildings, art in general or the Eastern Question Association, within the much broader social perspective that opened before him as he committed himself to the working class and to revolutionary socialism by joining H.M. Hyndman's Democratic Federation in 1883. Oxford was bound up with Morris's socialism in a curious way right from the very start, for it may just possibly – as May Morris asserts – have been on the same day in January 1883 that he heard he was elected Honorary Fellow of his old college, Exeter, *and* joined the Democratic Federation (*CW*, XIX, xv, but see also Salmon, 119). But Morris was determined that the connection between the two would be a lot less coincidental, and a good deal more public and controversial, than that. In the first days of July he and Burne-Jones were in Oxford being feted as new Fellows of their college; four months later Morris would return alone to declare himself a militant socialist at what may well be his single most famous or notorious public lecture.

'North Oxford in the 1880s was all Morris', asserts Fiona MacCarthy flamboyantly, basing her assertion on the *Daily Telegraph*'s obituary of

Morris in 1896: 'when married tutors dawned upon the academic world [after 1877], all their wives religiously clothed their walls in Norham-gardens and Bradmore road with Morrisian designs of clustering pomegranates' (MacCarthy, 413). Some advanced colleges were making similar aesthetic choices: University College ordered Morris wallpaper in 1879, while Brasenose in 1885 ordered both wallpaper and Persian glazed tiles for fireplaces from the Firm (*HUO*, VII, 2, 750). Yet even if Oxford middle-class interior decoration were as thoroughly Morrisian as the *Daily Telegraph* suggested, this was not, by the early 1880s, the kind of influence Morris most wanted to exert in his beloved city. The challenge for him now, as a public speaker, was to take his Oxford audiences from Arthurian poetry and floral wallpaper designs to revolutionary socialism, persuading them to cross that metaphorical 'river of fire' which he himself had traversed just a few years earlier (*CW*, XXII, 131–2). This was a tall order indeed, in class terms; yet, as we shall see, for a brief moment in the early part of the decade it looked as if such a convergence of Oxford and socialism might just be possible. We shall see how carefully Morris framed his socialist appeal in accessible Oxonian terms in his first great lecture there of November 1883; and the University at that moment was, as I shall demonstrate, unusually open to issues of working-class poverty and oppression, unusually receptive to political remedies to the left of traditional mainstream Liberalism.

On Wednesday 14 November 1883 William Morris announced to the Oxford audience who had assembled to hear him speak on 'Art and Democracy': 'I am "one of the people called Socialists"' (*CW*, XXIII, 172). When he made the same announcement, in a repetition of the lecture to an audience of eight hundred at Cambridge a few weeks later, 'a storm of mingled hisses and applause compelled him to pause for some minutes' (*Christian Socialist*, January 1884, 125). The Oxford response to the same declaration seems to have been altogether less equivocal. In a lecture which, according to the *Oxford Magazine*, was generally 'listened to with great attention and frequently applauded', Morris eventually announced that 'He himself was one of those people called Socialists (applause)' (*OM*, 21 November 1883, 386). We can attribute this warm welcome to Morris's remark to what W.T. Stead, reviewing the lecture for the *Pall Mall Gazette*, termed 'the changed spirit which has come over Oxford in recent years' (*PMG*, 15 November 1883, 4). Certainly at a later point in the speech, as Morris attacked capitalism for despoiling the architectural and natural environments, Stead noted that 'he had his audience with him'.

J.W. Mackail gives a terse helpful sketch in his biography:

> Social questions, under the stimulating influence of Arnold Toynbee and his disciples, had at that time risen to the first place among the intellectual interests of younger Oxford. Toynbee's recent death had only given a fresh impulse to the movement. The so-called University Settlements were in the air. Social reform was the current subject of discussion in College debating societies and filled the pages of the Oxford magazines. Mr. Henry George had lectured at Oxford ... and been received with a studied incivility which aroused a strong reaction in his favour. (Mackail, II, 117–18)

What Mackail does not mention here, however, is how personally close he was to these developments. For as a young Fellow at Balliol, he had published a poem about Toynbee in the wake of the latter's premature death at the age of thirty in March 1883: 'For a soul more pure and beautiful our eyes/ Shall never see again' (Kadish, 222).

In his biography of John Ruskin, Tim Hilton notes how powerful was 'the idea that a modern Oxford had been born in the early 1880s' (Hilton, 738). Sir Arthur Quiller-Couch, an undergraduate at Trinity College from 1882, gives a vivid evocation of the period which broadens out Mackail's account: 'In the autumn of 1882 the "aesthetic movement" had – in Oxford at any rate – almost run itself out of breath ... poetry and the arts for a while gave place in discussion to philosophy (notably that of T.H. Green) and social philanthropy – *The Bitter Cry of Outcast London*, Toynbee Hall, the crusades of W.T. Stead, etc. – a backwash from the prophetic preachings of Carlyle and Ruskin' (Quiller-Couch, 73–4). E.T. Cook, who as an undergraduate at New College had been an associate of Toynbee's and later became Ruskin's biographer and editor, went so far as to describe this 'practical interest in social questions' as 'the next Oxford movement' (Hilton, 837).

This latter notion achieved some currency at the time. In an article headed 'The New Oxford Movement' the *Oxford and Cambridge Undergraduate's Journal* announced that 'the glory of Oxford lies not in her matchless site ... but in the fact that she is pre-eminently of all English cities the mother of great movements', and continued: 'when the history of the latter half of the 19th century comes to be written, the most remarkable movement which the historian seems likely to be concerned with, will, we predict, be the rise of the social reformers' (22 November 1883, 110). The *Oxford Magazine* developed the issue. 'The question has been asked, "Is the new Oxford movement to be a socialistic one?" ... the answer must be distinctly, Yes! ... a new faith, with Professor Green for its founder, Arnold Toynbee for its martyr, and various societies for its propaganda, is alive amongst us' (21 November 1883, 384).

For the most significant of these Oxford reformers in the 1870s and early 1880s had indeed been T.H. Green and his disciple, Arnold Toynbee, though whether they were 'socialistic' or not is another matter entirely. Born in 1836, Green entered Balliol College, under Benjamin Jowett, in 1855, but the crucial intellectual turning point for him was his summer visits to Germany in 1862 and 1863. A close friend reported that Green was now 'full of German philosophy, politics, and the higher poetry', and we should also note that Green approved of Prussia because he found the artisans there 'free from the worse forms of socialism' (Richter, 90). Once back in Oxford, Green found his life's project at Balliol mapped out before him: to develop German idealist philosophy in ways that would underpin and extend his intuitive convictions in theology, politics and ethics. This would be no mean feat, as Melvin Richter has noted, 'for Green converted Philosophical Idealism, which had so often served as a rationale of conservatism, into something close to a practical programme for the left wing of the Liberal Party' (13). Though Green was an important figure in the professionalisation of philosophy in the later nineteenth century, he also saw it radiating out into all aspects of everyday life, and hence it is, as Richter and others have argued, that 'no word recurs more often in the work of Green and his followers than "citizenship"'(344).

We do not need to go into the technicalities of Green's philosophy: Oxford Idealism dominated the British philosophical scene from 1880 to 1914 and then fell into almost complete historical invisibility. But the social conclusions Green drew from it were an important force in articulating a shift from 'old' to 'new' liberalism. His lecture on 'Liberal

Legislation and Freedom of Contract', delivered at Leicester in 1880, was a crucial statement. Green here distinguished three phases of Liberal struggle: first, a political battle against aristocratic privilege; second, an economic struggle against protectionism; and now, in the present, a third phase devoted to a struggle for 'social freedoms'. This historical model also entailed a theoretical redefinition of the notion of 'freedom', which was no longer to be construed merely as the negative or primitive sense of 'being left alone' but rather as the 'positive power of doing or enjoying something worth doing or enjoying' (Vincent, 539). In enhancing such positive freedoms, state action might well play a crucial role, and we can thus see how Green is pushing liberalism beyond its earlier, laisser-faire manifestation towards what would become the more statist and welfare-orientated liberalism of the early twentieth century.

Green's general social precepts were given particular force in the minds of his pupils by his own devoted life of citizenship. He was active in the temperance movement, was a key spokesperson for the wider extension of university education, campaigned for the admission of women to Oxford, played a key role in founding Oxford Boys' High School and served as an assistant commissioner to Lord Taunton's schools inquiry commission. He also worked for his local Liberal Party and served on the Oxford town council as a Liberal member from 1875, being the first don to be actually elected to it rather than appointed by the University. However, heart trouble, in evidence from 1876, curtailed Green's practical reforming activities, and he died prematurely in his mid-forties in 1882.

A whole host of Oxonian memoirs testifies to the formative impact that Green's personality and thought had on the next generation of earnest and socially committed young men (and some women), both Liberal and Christian Socialist. But of all these disciples none is more crucial to Oxford than Arnold Toynbee; for Toynbee, much more explicitly than his mentor, attempts to refurbish liberalism so that it can cope with the revolutionary socialist challenge of the early 1880s. Toynbee died in March 1883, just one year after Green himself, at the tragically early age of thirty. At which point, as Alon Kadish notes, a whole machinery of mythologisation went into motion: 'Shortly after his death Toynbee came to be identified with two popular late Victorian middle-class images: the prophet and, to a larger extent, the martyr ... His martyrdom even assumed some of the trappings of iconolatry' (Kadish, 218, 222) – a process in which J.W. Mackail's own obituary poem clearly partakes. Here, for instance, is its second stanza:

> Goodbye; one star for us
> Is fallen; one hope has found its period.
> And while we turn to meet the drearier day,
> That sweet and gentle spirit, far away,
> With radiant face and eyes made luminous
> Looks in the face of God. (*OM*, 18 March 1883, 153)

Mackail's lumbering elegy, with its epigraph from Dante and its implied comparisons of Toynbee to Hector, Pallas, Lycidas and Astrophel, gives us twenty-three stanzas of such lofty and edifying generalities; it learnedly touches on all the conventions of the English elegy without once giving us any real sense of what its subject was actually like.

We need therefore to avoid this solemn glamorising of Toynbee and take a rather more sceptical and politically hard-nosed view of his life's work and influence. In his own meticulous study, Kadish argues that 'the story of his short life consists of a number of seemingly unrelated and somewhat ineffective endeavours', which included church reform, adult education, Oxford local politics and, most important for our purposes, 'an almost frantic attempt to salvage the crumbling alliance of the working classes and liberalism' (Kadish, ix).

Born in 1852, Toynbee went up to Oxford in January 1873, initially to Pembroke College but, after a bout of serious ill health and at Benjamin Jowett's doing, to Balliol from Hilary term 1875. In 1874 he joined John Ruskin's road-building project in Ferry Hinksey along with close friends like Alfred Milner, ending up as a foreman of one of the work parties. But though Ruskin may have turned the young man's attention to social problems, the latter's enduring liberalism meant that he was never at any point a Ruskin disciple. Toynbee absorbed from T.H. Green the principle of individual civic responsibility, which he put into practice in his undergraduate years both by tutoring trainee teachers and, in summer 1875, by spending a stint in London's East End to experience social conditions there at first hand. After taking a Pass degree, he was appointed as tutor to the probationers for the India Civil Service at Balliol, a post which established him in Oxford for the rest of his brief life.

As Toynbee's social and economic thought clarified itself, so we can see one single pressing political project emerge from his assorted activities in church reform, adult education, the co-operative movement, and municipal politics: the desire to take liberalism beyond its early, classic free trade and self-help phase to the point where it became socially radical enough to serve as an alternative to emerging socialism. In a lecture entitled 'Are Radicals Socialists?' delivered in early 1882 Toynbee dismissed what he termed 'German socialists' who clamoured for revolution as the only means to bring about social justice; for in his view 'the changes that German socialists thought could only be accomplished by a revolution had been gradually accomplished in England by continuous, peaceful progress' (Kadish, 119). Elasticating the term 'socialism', he eventually concludes that a new liberalism of cautious state intervention rather than laisser-faire meant that 'the Radical party has committed itself to a socialist programme' (120).

By the early 1880s Toynbee was turning his attention to the American reformer Henry George, whose theory of land nationalisation as expounded in his *Progress and Poverty* (1879) was in Toynbee's view getting a worrying grip on working-class organisations in both England and Ireland. In 1883 he gave two Oxford lectures on the subject to the Palmerston Club, a Liberal undergraduate society founded in 1877, but clearly felt that he needed to confront his enemy on its own terrain, in the working-class organisations of London itself. His Balliol contemporary, Alfred Milner, had given six talks on socialism in the East End in December 1882, and 'it is likely that Toynbee and Milner, as well as some of their closer associates such as Grey, regarded their lectures as part of a collective effort to stem the growth of revolutionary socialism by furnishing a sufficiently attractive alternative' (Kadish, 214). Toynbee's London lectures were initially to have taken place under the auspices of the Democratic Federation, but H.M. Hyndman vetoed this. In the event, they went ahead at Saint Andrew's Hall on 11 and 18 January 1883, just as William Morris was decisively committing himself to socialism by joining the Federation. According to Toynbee, Morris need not have bothered to do so. For liberalism had in effect transcended itself: 'the era of free trade and free contract is gone, and the era of administration has begun'. In Toynbee's view, Gladstone's Irish Land Act of 1881 had, beyond the latter's avowed conscious purpose, 'committed the Radical party to a socialist programme', where socialism was defined as the extension of state protection to the working class. Thus it was that, 'without revolution and without socialism, in the continental sense, we shall be able to do something towards that better distribution of wealth which we all desire to see' (206–7). At the second lecture Toynbee was given a very rough ride by his working-class audience, with some brutal comments from a 'Mr Kitts', who may just possibly be the Frank Kitz who was later an important colleague of Morris's in the Socialist League. He was taken from the lecture to his mother-in-law's house in Wimbledon in a state of nervous collapse from which he never recovered, and thus from March 1883 were born those myths of Toynbee's self-sacrificing martyrdom to the cause of social improvement.

Arnold Toynbee may have done Morris and the Democratic Federation a favour by turning the thoughts of Oxford undergraduates to social issues, but he had clearly also been a powerful and persuasive opponent of the socialists. At the very moment when Morris was trying in his earliest socialist writings in *Justice* to win over the Radical wing of the Liberal Party for revolutionary socialism, Toynbee was trying to refurbish and extend Radicalism to the point where it could repulse its left-wing challenger, claiming indeed to be more 'socialist' (in his elastic sense) than the Democratic Federation's 'German' version of the creed.

'The Dem: Fed: has made up its mind to have a shy at Oxford', Morris wrote cheerfully to Charles Faulkner on 17 October 1883 (*CL*, II, 235). Why had it done so at just this moment, one wonders? Did it see the deaths of Green in March 1882 and Toynbee in March 1883 as opening a gap in radical leadership at Oxford which it might aspire to fill and to inflect in a socialist direction, just as Ruskin's absence from the Sheldonian Theatre in 1879 had afforded Morris himself a chance to come to the fore as an architectural activist? He and Hyndman had received an invitation from the Russell Club, a society of Liberal undergraduates sympathetic to Radicalism, to speak in the hall of Faulkner's own college, University. The *Oxford and Cambridge Undergraduate's Journal* claims that 'Balliol Hall was refused to them' (22 November 1883, 105), so it may be that University College was not in fact the Russell Club's first choice of venue for this event.

But while the students may have been keen to hear Hyndman, the University authorities were not; Morris was acceptable, but 'Hyndman's doctrines were known to be revolutionary, and the methods he advocated were believed to be violent' (Mackail, II, 119). In a second letter to Faulkner, Morris offered a string of arguments to be used in an effort to persuade the Master of University, James Franck Bright, to change his mind: that he, Morris, was no less of a socialist than Hyndman, that he too intended to speak as a delegate of the Democratic Federation, that Hyndman was, after all, a university-educated man and quite possibly less robust in his expression of socialist opinions than Morris himself. The appeal may have had some effect, as also may the appearance of Hyndman's article on poverty in London in the *Pall Mall Gazette* on 29 October. But while the Master may possibly have changed his mind, the college authorities as a whole did not, and it was therefore Morris alone who faced the audience in the hall of University College on 14 November. The silencing of Hyndman seems to have made Morris himself unwontedly cautious in composing his lecture, which, he worried aloud to Faulkner, 'isn't my best, have been too careful – I fear mealy-mouthed' (*CL*, II, 243). Such caution may even have extended to the sartorial code Morris adopted for this occasion; for Stephen Gwynne, who was present at the lecture as a student, remarks in his autobiography that Morris had 'assum[ed] against his usage a conventional garb' with 'white shirt front' instead of the blue flannel shirt and dark-indigo jacket he typically wore (Gwynne, 41). The claim needs to be taken with a pinch of salt, however, since other figures present, such as A.H. Hawkins, later recorded Morris as wearing his usual blue outfit.

If the college authorities were wary, Conservative students were organising a more forthright opposition to Morris's arrival among them. They organised a petition against allowing the hall of University College to be used for his lecture, which attracted the signatures of a majority of the undergraduates and was presented to the Master just before the event, and held a wine party as 'a sort of opposition entertainment' (MacColl, 1945).

Interestingly, Morris had paid a private visit to Oxford with his daughter Jenny just a few days earlier. Taking up 'our quarters at the Kings Arms as usual' on 8 and 9 November, they lunched with Ingram Bywater, met Charles Faulkner and presumably did a good deal of all-round sight-seeing (*CL*, II, 237). It is as if Morris knew the intensity of the political storm that was about to break over his head and wanted a few quiet moments with his invalid daughter in his old haunts, a last chance to see vicariously through Jenny's eyes the wonderment that the grey city had instilled in him as an undergraduate. What would he have wanted to take his daughter to look at on a one-day tour of the city? The answer to this question is presumably given in Morris's 'Oxford list', which alas now no longer exists. In a brief set of 'Recollections of William Morris', published in *Artist* in 1897, the anonymous author gives a vivid account of a visit he and a friend made by bicycle to Morris in Kelmscott Manor, and continues: 'returning from Kelmscott, we passed a long day in Oxford, having been previously furnished by Morris with a list of the things that we should see in a day' ('Recollections', 62). However, he goes into no further detail about what it was that list contained, so our chance to see, in miniature and all at once, what Morris considered the chief tourist treasures of Oxford has vanished for good.

For William Morris to lecture at his old university on socialism was indeed, as both contemporary and later commentators have stressed, a deeply symbolic event in his political evolution, a way of publicly propelling himself still further across the 'river of fire' that separated middle-class liberalism, radicalism or philanthropy from revolutionary socialism. Yet the symbolism of the event has been cranked up in many later retellings of this occasion to the point where it verges, even in Morris's most serious scholars, on sheer mythology; so some preliminary sorting out of the basic facts of the lecture will here prove worthwhile.

The mythologizing begins early on, with May Morris referring to 'an address on Socialism delivered in Oxford with John Ruskin in the chair' in her Introduction to volume XXIII of the *Collected Works* (xij–xiij). Later scholars such as E.P. Thompson, A.L. Morton, Jack Lindsay and

Philip Henderson have all followed May Morris on this point, and even Morris's most careful recent biographer asserts that 'Ruskin, by now aged sixty-three and looking more than ever like an ancient prophet, was in his second term of office as Slade Professor of Art and was in the chair' (MacCarthy, 477).

John Ruskin was certainly in the hall of University College as Morris delivered 'Art Under Plutocracy', as he had not been in the Sheldonian Theatre during the St Mark's protest meeting of 1879; but he was *not* in the chair. Why, then, should Morris commentators, all the way from May Morris onwards, so stubbornly seek to put him there? Presumably because the sense of a generational transfer of values from the ailing art critic to his younger, more robust and now overtly socialist disciple is thereby made all the stronger; and this impulse was still active in Morris himself, who had invited Ruskin to join the Democratic Federation earlier that year. Morris refers very positively to Ruskin's teachings during the course of his lecture, above all to the doctrine that 'ART IS MAN'S EXPRESSION OF HIS JOY IN LABOUR' (*CW*, XXIII, 173), and the effect of this invocation is made all the more intense if Ruskin is indeed presiding over the event as chairman.

However, he was not; so who actually was? A second legend has grown up here, which substitutes one Oxford luminary for another. That meticulous Morris scholar Norman Kelvin tells us in a footnote to the *Collected Letters* that the meeting 'was chaired by Benjamin Jowett, the Master of Balliol … Morris's lecture … scandalized Jowett, who said he would never have agreed to be chairman had he known what Morris was going to say' (*CL*, II, 235). Nicholas Salmon, the most careful of all Morris critics, while correctly pointing out in his *Chronology* that Ruskin 'was not the chairman as has often been stated', goes on to declare that 'the chairman, Benjamin Jowett, was scandalized by Morris's remarks' (Salmon, 127). Jowett remains a well-known representative Oxford figure to this day, so again, if he is in the chair, this may be presumed to add lustre and drama to Morris's great political break with his alma mater.

But, in fact, neither Ruskin nor Jowett chaired on this occasion, and there is indeed some doubt as to whether Jowett was even present in the hall; none of the contemporary accounts of Morris's lecture identifies him as being present. The answer we want – the bare, colourless historical fact behind the later mythologizing – is given in the *Oxford Magazine*'s detailed report of Morris's talk, which notes that 'the Chairman, Mr A. H. Hawkins, briefly introduced the lecturer' (21 November 1883, 386). The *Oxford and Cambridge Undergraduate's Journal* confirms this: 'Mr. Hawkins, Balliol, presided' (22 November 1883, 115). Hawkins may not ever have achieved the intellectual eminence of Ruskin or Jowett, but he is not a complete literary nonentity either. Like Morris, he was educated at Marlborough College and he then went up to Balliol in October 1881, where he threw himself into the University political scene: 'I was a great Radical and ... signified the same by often sporting a red tie and by wearing my hair ... rather long' (Hope, 58). He played a prominent role in the Russell Club and became President of the Oxford Union in 1886. But it is for his subsequent career as a novelist, under the pseudonym Anthony Hope, that Hawkins is best remembered today, and particularly for his 1894 novel *The Prisoner of Zenda*, set in the fictional kingdom of Ruritania. The book was so popular in its own day that it was dramatised in 1895, followed up by Hope himself with a prequel and sequel, gave the word 'Ruritania' to the language in general, and was dramatised several times for television in the twentieth century. So it was a notable talent in the making who chaired William Morris as he prepared to tackle Oxford on socialism in November 1883.

It is time, finally, to turn to the lecture itself, and it is striking to see how strong the consensus is about the value of this piece: 'this is one of his great lectures' (MacCarthy, 477); 'one of Morris's most splendid lectures ... has since become a classic' (Henderson, 256–8). If 'Art under Plutocracy' indeed deserves such plaudits, one wonders why Morris chose not to include it in the collection of his socialist lectures, *Signs of Change*, in 1888. The reason, surely, is its intense specificity to its occasion. Oxford here is not just the venue for the lecture, but an integral part of its argument too, and Morris is very alert indeed to this dialectical interplay between theme and location. So rhetorically sensitive is his text to its audience in University College hall in November 1883 – the date as well as the place will matter – that it could not be effectively offered as part of the more general political case that Morris wanted to make in *Signs of Change* (though that collection has its own reference to Oxford in 'The Aims of Art').

The sensitivity to local context comes through in the very opening moments of the talk. Morris's offer to 'take counsel' with his audience over contemporary hindrances to art at once evokes an earnest intimacy, a shared and sustained effort of understanding; and he goes on to ventriloquise possible audience responses to his argument. 'Some of you here may think that the hindrances in the way are none, or few, and easy to be swept aside. You will say that there is on many sides much knowledge of the history of art, and plenty of taste for it' (*CW*, XXIII, 164). Such views are reasonable enough, but only within the framework of a truncated view of art which Morris then proceeds to explode in one of his great and defining affirmations:

> first I must ask you to extend the word art beyond those matters which are consciously works of art, to take in not only painting and sculpture, and architecture, but the shapes and colours of all household goods, nay, even the arrangement of the fields for tillage and pasture, the management of towns and of our highways of all kinds; in a word, to extend it to the aspect of all the externals of our life. (164–5)

Once art has been redefined in this way, then the physical environment in which the lecture itself takes place – its 'externals', the town and highways amidst which it is delivered – at once becomes crucial to its argument. Thus Morris's question as to what kind of account he and his contemporaries will be able to give to those who come after them of their dealings with the earth 'may well seem a solemn one when it is asked here in Oxford, amidst sights and memories which we older men at least regard with nothing short of love' (165).

Morris's argument keeps coming back to Oxford, long before he offers any declaration of socialist commitment. A theoretical definition of the distinction between Intellectual and Decorative arts moves into a historical retrospect of the creative interaction that existed between them in 'the times of art'. Once that benign linkage is sundered, decorative art decays rapidly, so to reactivate in his audience the memory of what it once was Morris offers the following finely crafted appeal:

> Think, I beg you, to go no further back in history, of the stately and careful beauty of S. Sophia at Constantinople, of the golden twilight of S. Mark's at Venice; of the sculptured cliffs of the great French

cathedrals; of the quaint and familiar beauty of our own minsters; nay, go through Oxford streets and ponder on what is left us there unscathed by the fury of the thriving shop and the progressive college; or wander some day through some of the out-of-the-way villages ... within twenty miles of Oxford; and you will surely see that the loss of decorative art is a grievous loss to the world. (169)

No doubt there were a good many veterans of the 1879 Sheldonian St Mark's meeting in Morris's audience in November 1883; their cultural sympathies are reactivated as Morris resituates that earlier SPAB campaign within the wider social struggle he is now envisaging. A continuity is asserted between the glories of S. Sophia and St Mark's and the gentler domestic beauties of the 'grey city', and even the academic culture of country walking, so strong in Victorian Oxford, is drawn into the argument here.

Not only the built environment but Nature too suffers grievously at the hands of 'civilization', Morris asserts. London and Manchester swallow up the countryside around them at a prodigious rate, and every little market town hurries to imitate them, with the result that 'the well of art [Nature] is poisoned at its source'. At which point Morris returns to Oxford for the third time in the first half of his lecture:

Need I speak to you of the wretched suburbs that sprawl all round our fairest and most ancient cities? Must I speak to you of the degradation that has so speedily befallen this city, still the most beautiful of them all; a city which, with its surroundings, would, if we had had a grain of common sense, have been treated like a most precious jewel ... I am old enough to know how we have treated that jewel; as if it were any common stone kicking about on the highway, good enough to throw at a dog. When I remember the contrast between the Oxford of to-day and the Oxford which I first saw thirty years ago, I wonder I can face the misery (there is no other word for it) of visiting it, even to have the honour of addressing you to-night. (171)

We have seen that the *Oxford Magazine* attributed the Magdalen Bridge widening to the transport requirements of the rapidly increasing suburbs of Oxford, and though the term 'suburb' does not occur, as far I can tell, in SPAB's campaign on the issue, the social process itself was clearly strongly on Morris's mind. May Morris quotes a remark of her father's to the effect that Oxford was 'desecrated by the invasion of the married Don' (*CW*, XXIII, xiv), which is presumably a reference to the statute of 1877 which allowed college Fellows to keep their Fellowships when they married, and which at once led to substantial domestic building growth along the Banbury and Woodstock Roads. The great irony for Morris himself is that, though his decorative products were highly popular among the North Oxford middle class, that suburb itself was part of the web of social processes that were threatening his 'jewel' of a city. And North Oxford was only one of the five Oxford suburbs (the others being to the east, south and west of the city, and Jericho) whose rapid growth was the reason that the city's population increased from just over 24,000 in 1841 to just under 41,000 in 1881 (Graham, 2).

The contrast which Morris proceeds to draw between the Oxford of the 1880s and the Oxford of his undergraduate days thirty years earlier is a persistent one in his writings; indeed, it almost constitutes a distinctive mini-genre in its own right, the Morrisian Oxford elegy. It is persuasive and plangent, and no doubt both Morris's original audience in University College hall and most of his subsequent readers have been won over by it. But it is a very one-sided way of telling that particular historical story, and we ourselves perhaps need to take a fuller, more dialectical view – one with which Morris, as a Marxist and not just an architectural activist, might well have agreed in other contexts. For the Oxford of the early 1850s, though it may have been architecturally delectable in a way that only Rouen among medieval cities could match, was also notoriously unhealthy. There had been cholera epidemics in 1832, 1849 and 1854, the last of which had impacted upon Morris's own student career, and Anthony Howe gives us a helpful synopsis of the scale of the problems: 'By the 1850s the medical community had provided a clear critique of the public health hazards of Oxford – higher than average mortality as a result of closed courts, overcrowded homes among the poor, large open drains, irregularly emptied cesspools, as well as insalubrious lodging-houses and pigsties' (Whiting, 23). The modernisation of Oxford, which Morris so often deplores from a SPAB viewpoint, had at least had some impact on these severe health problems, with Dean Liddell and Dr Henry Acland, who themselves stood on the Society's side over St Mark's in the Sheldonian in 1879, playing particularly admirable roles on the public health front. Urban modernisation in the case of Oxford as of any other city was thus a double-edged process, bringing benefits as well as blight, a fact which Marxism, as a dialectical mode of thinking that sees capitalism as both the best and worst thing that has ever happened to humanity, should have no particular difficulty in accepting.

Having so strongly drawn his Oxonian audience into his discourse in the early sections of his November 1883 lecture, Morris can then proceed to a sharper politics, moving finally beyond a SPAB-style appeal to 'cultivated men', to socialism proper. The destructive force of 'civilization' is now specified as belonging to just 'one phase of it ... the system of competition in the production and exchange of the means of life', or capitalism in short (*CW*, XXIII, 172). It is this economic system which has caused the architectural havoc that Oxford, as a medieval city, both challenges and bears grievous witness to; and Morris can thus finally declare 'I am "one of the people called Socialists"' (172). But no sooner has he done so than he gives his social thinking a distinctively Oxonian inflection. Intellectual art cannot be separated from the wider society, from the conditions of labour of the mass of mankind, because ultimately 'ART IS MAN'S EXPRESSION OF HIS JOY IN LABOUR. If those are not Professor Ruskin's words they embody at least his teaching on this subject' (173). The appeal back to Ruskin's authority is a familiar enough move in Morris's prose, but made as it was here, in the physical presence of the Slade Professor himself, it must have had unusual force for Morris's University College audience. No sooner has the disturbing and revolutionary term 'socialism' made its appearance in Morris's discourse than it is shrewdly folded back into a more familiar tradition of Ruskinian social critique.

Morris's lecture is strongly located not only in its place but also in its time of delivery; for it refers several times in its second half to 'the poor wretches, the news of whom we middle-class people are just now receiving with such naïf wonder and horror' (179). The reference here, in a lecture delivered on 14 November 1883, is to the Congregational Minister Andrew Mearns's vivid pamphlet, *The Bitter Cry of Outcast London: An Inquiry into the Condition of the Abject Poor*, which had been

published in mid-October of that year. Mearns's work was strongly pro-
moted by W.T. Stead in the *Pall Mall Gazette* and by the *Daily News*, and
made a significant impact in Oxford itself. Shortly after its publication
the Reverend Montagu Butler brandished a copy during a sermon he
preached at St Mary's Church and made a passionate plea for Oxford to
turn its talents to the appalling working-class housing problems Mearns
had so effectively exposed (Mearns, 24). 'The "Bitter Outcry" has had a
more general reading than any such pamphlet for years', remarked the
Oxford and Cambridge Undergraduate's Journal (22 November 1883, 105),
and Davey Biggs, an undergraduate at St Johns College at the time,
noted just how pervasive the pamphlet was; for as students 'loitered
in the College barge waiting their turn to be "tubbed" they found
the dressing-room table littered with copies of *The Bitter Cry of Outcast
London*' (Ball, 205). Morris himself later explicitly acknowledged the
impact of the pamphlet, though with a shrewd sense of how short-lived
its influence among the middle class had been, when he asked in *Commonweal* in July 1888: 'What has become of the "Bitter Cry" and all the
fashionable slumming which followed it?' (*PW*, 378).

Towards the end of his lecture Morris turns back to Oxford again
– not to its architecture this time but to the body of cultivated men,
to borrow that crucial term of his SPAB campaigning, which constitutes
the University. He invites them to throw in their lot with revolutionary
socialism, though he knows how disablingly deep is that 'dread of or-
ganization ... which, as it is very common in England generally, is more
common among highly cultivated people, and, if you will forgive the
word, most common in our ancient universities' (*CW*, XXIII, 190). But
if they could renounce their class identity and embrace the Democratic
Federation, the cultural benefits would be mutual; for 'as you help us
in our work-a-day business towards the success of the cause, instil into
us your superior wisdom, your superior refinement, and you in your
turn may be helped by the courage and hope of those who are not so
completely wise and refined' (191). For in the revolutionary movement,
it would seem, the old fissuring of Intellectual and Decorative Arts, or
of mental and manual labour, can be overcome in a quite new way.

I have sought to show, then, how rooted 'Art under Plutocracy' is in
its Oxford location. The deictics of the talk – 'there are but few, at least

here' (185, my stress) – refer not just to any lecture hall but specifically to Oxford as both city and university, while the appeal throughout to a shared class identity – 'the more advanced in opinion of our own class' (181) – refers more precisely to the cultivated men to whom SPAB had appealed with such mixed results in 1879 and 1881, and of whom Oxford could muster so many. Yet the very strength of Morris's lecture as a local intervention disqualifies it, as he himself clearly realised, as a general statement of socialism, which is presumably why it could find no place in *Signs of Change* in 1888. Yet we can see in retrospect that this talk brings together three strands of his thought – conservationist campaigns in Oxford and elsewhere, a Ruskinian celebration of medievalism and joy in labour, and the new socialist view of history – with a depth and eloquence that Morris rarely matched elsewhere in his writings.

After the lecture Morris took questions from the floor. These are not reported in any of the contemporary newspaper accounts, but Anthony Hawkins later recalled:

> I am afraid he did not enjoy the meeting much. His speech went well, but afterwards two or three political economy dons heckled him severely on points of detail, and it was evident that these pin-pricks rather puzzled and distressed him. He seemed not to understand how men could meet his beautiful vision of a regenerated society with such petty cavilling. (Hope, 82)

There has been at least as much mythologising of the end of Morris's talk as there has been of its beginning. Here, for example, is Aymer Vallance, who in his 1897 study of Morris claims that 'in concluding the lecture [Morris] as a practical step, advised his audience to marry, as it would be called, "beneath" them in order to break down the existing social barriers between class and class. Fancy that in a College Hall!' (Vallance, 233). One can hardly imagine Morris publicly offering his own unhappy marriage with Jane Burden, who was the daughter of an Oxford ostler, as a model for social action, and it is entirely unlikely that he said anything of the sort.

John Ruskin's role at Morris's lecture has in fact been doubly mythologised, first by placing him in the chair at its beginning, and second by having him salvage a difficult situation at the end of the talk. Morris's appeal to his audience to join the Democratic Federation may well have shocked the dignitaries on the platform with him, and here is Fiona MacCarthy's colourful account of what happened next:

> As Morris ended speaking there was a deathly hush. The Master, Dr Bright, rose in an anguish of embarrassment to say that the college had no idea that Mr Morris was the agent of any Socialist propaganda. What they had intended was simply to give an eminent man the opportunity of expressing his opinions on art under democracy, a subject with which Mr Morris was 'unusually well acquainted, and a knowledge of which, in the existing condition of social questions in England, was a most desirable part of the education of every young man'.
> Ruskin got to his feet and smoothed the situation over. (MacCarthy, 478–9)

This account, which fits with that offered by various other scholars, is certainly attractive in the benign centrality it accords to Ruskin, but it is completely incorrect because Ruskin actually spoke *before*, and not after, Dr Bright.

It is therefore crucial to establish the bald sequence of events at the close of Morris's lecture, which we can readily do by turning to the detailed account in the *Oxford Magazine*:

> The Warden of Keble proposed a vote of thanks to Mr. Morris, and Professor Ruskin, who was received with enthusiastic applause, seconded it ... The vote was carried by acclamation, and Mr. Morris briefly responded.
> The Chairman then proposed the thanks of the Russell Club to the Master and Fellows of University College for the use of the Hall. The Master replied in a few well-chosen words. He took the opportunity of explaining that when the Hall was lent to the Club, it was not known that Mr. Morris was the agent of any socialist propaganda. (*OM*, 387)

Ruskin's response to the Warden of Keble's proposal is reported as follows in the *Pall Mall Gazette*:

> Mr. Ruskin, whose appearance was the signal for immense enthusiasm, speaking of the lecturer as 'the great conceiver and doer, the man at once a poet, an artist, and a workman, and his old and dear friend,' said that he agreed with him in 'imploring the young men who were being educated here, and their wives, to seek, in true unity and love

for one another, the best direction for the great forces which, like an evil aurora, were lighting the world, and thus to bring about the peace which passeth all understanding'. (*PMG*, 4)

This may not have been quite all that Ruskin said. According to the *Oxford Magazine*, he 'pronounced a benediction over his pupil and the audience, joining as he said (with a characteristic twist of Milton's lines), in the "wail of a disturbed *discontent*" sung for the time before the "sapphire-coloured throne"' (384), before he moved on to the aurora simile reported by the *Pall Mall Gazette*. But whatever the extent of his contribution and whatever the enthusiasm for it in the hall on the night, his later admirers remain unimpressed by it. The editors of his collected works note wryly that Ruskin ended up 'by some transition of thought no longer recoverable, with a description of a sunset' (Cook and Wedderburn, XXXIII, 390), and Tim Hilton is a good deal more forthright, describing Ruskin's entire speech (as far as we can reconstruct it) as 'emollient and meaningless remarks' (Hilton, 747). So though Ruskin was present in University College hall, as he had not been in the Sheldonian in 1879, he remained – to those who could read the symptoms – but the ghost of his former self.

Fiona MacCarthy colourfully asserts that the Master of University, Dr James Franck Bright, was in 'an anguish of embarrassment' after Morris's lecture; the *Oxford Magazine* coolly notes that he offered a 'few well-chosen words'. Which account is nearer the mark? We do know that Dr Bright had a stammer – 'he stammered a little at all times' (Gwynne, 41) – so the fact that his speech was falteringly delivered need not necessarily indicate the extreme emotion that MacCarthy surmises. The *Oxford and Cambridge Undergraduate's Journal* cites Bright as saying that Morris, as an eminent man, had been invited to give 'his view of what ought to be done in the crisis to which human history was evidently tending' (116), which suggests that Bright himself had been touched by the 'bitter cry' of contemporary social distress that was making such an impact on Oxford in the early 1880s; he may not therefore have been so entirely horrified by Morris's social views as later commentators have tended to conclude. He was after all certainly identified with liberal causes in Oxford: he wanted to open theological degrees to other than Church of England members, and he had just become president of the Association for Promoting the Education of Women. Moreover, Arthur Quiller-Couch later suggested that Bright was simply protecting his back in University College hall, given the intense media interest in Morris's talk: he 'explained that he ... felt himself out of sympathy with Mr. Morris's opinions. The disclaimer was made, I suppose, to satisfy the press' (cited in Faulkner, 396). The Master of University may therefore have been playing a shrewder game than Morris scholars have supposed.

What did Morris himself make of Dr Bright's remarks? Stephen Gwynne declares that 'Morris at any time was choleric and his face flamed red over his white shirt front: he probably thought he had conceded enough by assuming against his usage a conventional garb' (Gwynne, 41). As I have noted above, Gwynne's memoirs are of uncertain reliability, yet such an intense response would indeed be consistent with our general sense of Morris's inflammable temper.

We need to move beyond reactions to Morris's talk in the hall itself to track down, as best we can, responses to it in the days and weeks following. Morris's own immediate response, next morning, seems to have been panic about losing the text of his lecture; for D.S. MacColl wrote to his sister that 'next day I was assailed by the Secretary (Kalisch) as Mr. Morris said that a tall dark man with a moustache had taken his MS. for the Oxford Magazine. This appears to have been a dream, as it was found in his pocket after all' (MacColl, 1944). It appears that Morris's general 'terror' at returning to Oxford in these years had suddenly displaced itself onto his lecture text and assailed him in unusually severe form.

John Ruskin responded to Morris's talk a second time, in his own lecture on the 'Hillside' as represented in the work of Copley Fielding given just a few days later, where he argued that

> the significant change which Mr. Morris made in the title of his recent
> lecture, from Art and *Democracy*, to Art and *Plutocracy*, strikes at
> the root of the whole matter; and with wider sweep of blow than he
> permitted himself to give his words. The changes which he so deeply
> deplored, and so grandly resented, in this once loveliest city, are due
> wholly to the fact that her power is now dependent on the Plutocracy
> of Knowledge instead of its Divinity. (Cook and Wedderburn, XXXIII,
> 390 and n)

What can we say of the reaction of Morris's student audience to his lecture? Writing after Morris's death in 1896, Arthur Quiller-Couch cast his mind back to the 1883 talk and in rather satirical vein recalled: 'We were babes, and he gave us the strongest meat. We came for help over rudimentary difficulties, and he stormed at us and threatened. We were choked by alternate doses of mediaevalism and crude Socialism ... For some weeks afterwards a few enthusiasts tried to persuade their comrades that the social problem could be solved by importing another Black Death and enrolling the survivors in Guilds' (Faulkner, 396). Amusing though this last remark is, it does suggest that socialist sympathisers at the university made at least some effort to organise themselves in the weeks after Morris's lecture, though clearly nothing as well-defined as the Oxford Socialist League branch of 1885 came into being at this point.

Shortly after his Oxford lecture Morris wrote to Georgiana Burne-Jones: 'I have been living in a sort of storm of newspaper brickbats, to some of which I had to reply' (*CL*, II, 249). In fact, press response to his Oxford talk was far from uniformly hostile. The Oxford correspondent of the *Cambridge Review*, for instance, termed it 'a singularly forcible and eloquent denunciation of the evils of competition' (21 November 1883, 93). But it appears that Morris made a remark in his talk or in his answers to the subsequent questions which gave a serious hostage to fortune and was indeed swiftly pounced on in the local and national press by political opponents. The slippage, if that is indeed what it was, came as he announced Hyndman's follow-up lecture.

A letter in the *Pall Mall Gazette* from 'One of the Audience' took him sternly to task over this:

> Towards the close of his paper Mr. Morris informed us that it would be shortly followed by an address from Mr. Hyndman, expounding the economic bases of the 'reconstructive Socialism' which Mr. Morris and his friends wish to substitute for the existing 'devil-take-the-hindmost' system; 'for,' added the lecturer (I can only give the substance of his words), 'I do not myself claim to be versed in the economics of the principles we advocate.'

This admission, if Morris had in fact made it, was certainly very damaging to his case, as the *Gazette*'s correspondent proceeded to point out. For Morris had indeed argued that the artistic development of the nation depends upon its economic principles. And yet it is of these principles, which, according to his own assumption, are fundamental, that Mr. Morris confesses his ignorance ... He advocates changes which must affect the entire life of every person in these islands, and finishes by telling us that he does not know what he is talking about. (*PMG*, 16 November 1883, 2)

Had Morris used the alleged words or not? In his reply to the *Pall Mall Gazette* the next day, he admits that he cannot remember the actual words he employed in announcing Hyndman's lecture. The *Oxford and Cambridge Undergraduate's Journal*, in its article on 'The New Oxford Movement', asked contemptuously, 'what are we to think of the Radicals of Oxford when one of the more eminent of their apostles has to confess, in a public lecture-room, that he knows nothing of economics? To term the Radical of the day a dreamer of dreams, is flattery itself' (22 November 1883, 111). A letter in the *Oxford Magazine* pressed home the same point: 'he made his lecture in some sort a manifesto. And yet – in the face of this – he had to confess that he knew nothing of the reconstruction that is to come: he had to refer us to others who knew more' (21 November 1883, 396). It may well be that these accusations are part of a concerted attack by Morris's political opponents, yet it appears that he might after all have said something careless enough to let them fasten upon.

Morris tried to claw back the lost ground in his *Pall Mall Gazette* reply, arguing that 'an assertion of the economical basis of Socialism was at least implied all through my lecture if it was not formally stated.' But he had approached the economic issue, he freely admitted, as an artist. It was his enthusiastic admiration of medieval art at the start of his career and his subsequent defence of popular art which had led him into an inquiry into the economic bases of craftwork and art across the centuries, and had moved him to that fierce rejection of 'competitive commerce' which he had offered his audience in University College hall (*CL*, II, 247).

We occasionally catch fleeting glimpses of undergraduate response to Morris during his phase as a Democratic Federation activist at Oxford. Michael Sadler had gone up to Trinity College in 1880 to read Literae Humaniores, attended John Ruskin's 1883–4 lectures, and subsequently advanced Ruskinian ideals through his central role in the Oxford University Extension movement from 1885 onwards – though the eirenic and class-reconciliationist ideals of this movement hardly represented the kind of working-class education Morris was committed to. In Michaelmas term 1883 Sadler was living in digs with Leonard Huxley in Museum Cottage, and from there he wrote on 10 November describing

> Mr William Morris, with whom I had the privilege of smoking a pipe on Friday night. A little man with short legs and a small meerschaum, a tangled grey beard, high forehead, rough hair, and blue flannel shirt with a tie. A keen talker but slangy. Himself and his friends always 'chaps' – salmon fishing in an Iceland glacier stream 'tremendously jolly', Teuton excellence lying in their love of the 'rough and tumble hullabaloo of a battle', Romans slack because 'they didn't like fighting for its own sake don't you know?' I could hardly credit his having written the EARTHLY PARADISE. He is full of socialism and has become a political lecturer. (Sadleir, 45)

Sadler's letter just predates Morris's 'Art and Democracy' lecture on 14 November, so it perhaps is not surprising that it is still the latter's identity as poet which predominates here, just as it did in Oxford University's invitation to him in 1877 to become Professor of Poetry – the 'idle singer of an empty day' turning out, however, to be a good deal more forceful, both personally and politically, than the cultured melancholy of his verse had given Sadler reason to expect. We have noted above the *Cambridge Review*'s complaints about Morris's unpolished and colloquial manner in the Sheldonian in November 1879 and it appears that Sadler got a particularly intense dose of Morris in this vein.

Though the *Cambridge Review* was very positive about Morris's 1883 lecture, it did enter an important caveat: 'Mr. Morris did not enter on any constructive scheme, but referred us to Mr. Hyndman' (21 November 1883, 93). This is a reading strongly at odds with our own current sense of Morris, where it is precisely his passion and precision in offering constructive views of socialism – 'How We Might Live', 'A Factory As It Might Be' or even the full-blown utopia *News from Nowhere* itself – that makes him so distinctive and enduringly valuable to us. But clearly in these early days of the Democratic Federation propaganda Morris was uneasy about his own qualifications for holding forth on socialism and inclined to play a subaltern role to Hyndman himself. In his letter to Faulkner answering the Master of University College's objections to Hyndman, Morris argues that one surely ought to get one's socialism direct from the horse's mouth, from 'a man who is allowed by Socialists to be capable of giving a definite exposition of the whole doctrine, which as you know I am not capable of doing in a scientific & detailed way' (*CL*, II, 236). So it was that, after having been silenced in November, Hyndman at last got his chance to address Oxford in the Clarendon Assembly Rooms in late January 1884. The exact date of this event remains elusive. Eugene LeMire gives it as 27 January, on the basis of a report in the *Church Reformer*; but the *Oxford Magazine*, which one might regard as being closer to the occasion it is reporting, gives it as 30 January. Hyndman's topic now was, precisely, 'Constructive Socialism'. The hosts were again the Russell Club, and William Morris was also on the platform.

January 1884 was a crucial month for the public profile of the Democratic Federation. A donation of £300 from Edward Carpenter had allowed the organisation to start a weekly newspaper, *Justice*, whose first issue appeared on 19 January. Moreover, Hyndman and his colleagues had acquired and relaunched the moribund journal *To-Day*, whose first new-style issue also came out in January of this year. The Federation now had media through which it could reach both the working class and the middle-class intelligentsia, and it is in the context of this latter, more theoretical campaign that we must situate the visits to Oxford and Cambridge that Morris and Hyndman made in late January and early February 1884.

'Constructive Socialism' was certainly an unusual title for Hyndman to alight upon. His favoured adjective in these heady early years was 'revolutionary'. In 1881 he had published 'The Dawn of a Revolutionary Epoch' in the *Nineteenth Century*; in October 1883 he held forth on 'Revolutionary Socialism' in the *Pall Mall Gazette*; and he followed these up with an article on 'The Revolution of To-Day' in the first issue of the new Democratic Federation journal in January 1884. He there warns his readership that 'in five years we reach the date of 1889', and that this year – the one-hundredth anniversary of the French Revolution and the two-hundredth anniversary of the 'middle-class monarchical revolution of 1689' – will be the signal for the industrial workers to make their own, proletarian, revolution in Europe's cities (*To-Day*, January 1884, 23). In switching from 'revolutionary' to 'constructive' socialism for his Oxford lecture was Hyndman perhaps making a concession to his university hosts, toning down his fire-breathing rhetoric a fraction in order to secure the opportunity to appeal to undergraduate hearts and minds? And given how important the term 'constructive' is in Morris's own early socialist correspondence, where it comes up repeatedly to point a contrast with the merely destructive schemes of the anarchists, we might wonder whether it was not Morris himself who had urged the change of epithet upon Hyndman.

The meeting was again held under the auspices of the Russell Club, but this time at the Clarendon Assembly Rooms rather than University College. The Clarendon Hotel occupied what is today the Cornmarket frontage of the Clarendon Centre; it had been a coaching inn, known as the Star, for hundreds of years until it was taken over and renamed by the Clarendon Hotel Company in 1863 (the building was finally demolished in 1954 and replaced by Woolworths). Between three and four hundred people attended the event, mostly undergraduates, though with 'a fair sprinkling of graduates and ladies' too (*Church Reformer*, February 1884, 46). The Master of University College, James Bright, was in the audience, so he had clearly not been as traumatised by socialist views as some commentators on Morris's November 1883 lecture have made him out to be. The president of the Russell Club, the Rev. G. C. Fletcher, announced that the Club had planned to ask Hyndman to lecture in Michaelmas term 1883, but that 'it had been thought better to postpone the invitation to this term, owing to the plays which had created so much interest at the end of the previous term' (*Justice*, 16 February 1884, 7), which seems a graceful way of diplomatically slurring over the controversy caused by the University's manoeuvres to stop Hyndman's earlier talk.

Hyndman himself, most unwontedly for him, was nervous about the event. He and Morris had travelled up the day before and dined with Faulkner, and in his *Record of an Adventurous Life* he admits that he knew that Henry George's Oxford lecture on land nationalisation the week before had gone badly and that he anticipated similar problems for himself. In fact, Hyndman's memory, as he writes his autobiography in 1911, lets him down here. For Henry George's Oxford lecture, which was indeed an uproarious event, took place in March 1884 – that is, well after his own address to the Russell Club in January.

But however worried in advance Hyndman may have been about his Oxford reception, once at the podium the next day he very quickly metamorphosed back into the self-confident speaker he normally was: 'I had not spoken for ten minutes before I had the assurance to bend down and whisper to Morris, "I shall capture this lot"' (Hyndman, 354). And he does indeed seem to have won over his audience. *Justice* reports that 'at times they were carried away and burst out into loud applause' (7). Lest one suspect that the official organ of the Democratic Federation is seeing everything through rose-coloured spectacles, we can turn to the more sober *Church Reformer*, which confirms that 'the able Lecturer was attentively listened to, and the audience sometimes became quite enthusiastic' (46).

Hyndman began his lecture by asserting that socialism had a definite historical and economic theory, and by distancing himself from Henry George's nostrum of land nationalisation. He went on to expound socialist doctrine, with a historical sketch of the development from feudalism to machine industry and the factory system, with its immiseration of the working class, and with an account of the theory of surplus value, illustrated with extracts from Karl Marx and Thomas Hodgskin. Turning his attention to contemporary trade crises, he located their source in the fact that, though production was now socialised, exchange of goods remained subject to the anarchy of capitalist competition. Finally – turning genuinely 'constructive' at last – he proposed some specific collectivist measures: free schools and decent school dinners, state legislation over maximum hours of work and minimum wage levels, state administration of railways, mines, factories, shipping, even land nationalisation, though – in a parting swipe at Henry George – this was likely to 'be the last, not the first, change' (*OM*, 6 February 1884, 51).

Thereafter, in a decidedly subaltern role, William Morris spoke on socialism for the second time at his old university. *The Church Reformer* notes only that 'Mr. Morris followed in a kindly and all too short speech'

(46), and one wonders how much of a contrast with the tone and content of Hyndman's lecture the adjective 'kindly' implies here. Had Hyndman's talk, despite its title, come across after all as more destructive than constructive? The *Oxford Magazine* gives us rather more detail, in the light of which it appears that Morris's contribution may have been extempore rather than scripted, and that it was mostly a response to some of the objections to Hyndman's lecture lodged by A. Williams, a former president of the Russell Club. In what must have been an extensive reply, Williams challenged Hyndman on labour being the source of all value, disputed his figures on working-class incomes, objected to land nationalisation (though himself demanding several changes in current land laws), and declared stoutly that socialism fostered class hatred. At which point 'Mr. William Morris ... spoke, and declared that the aim of Socialism was to extinguish class hatreds by making the interests of all identical. The law of competition was that the man who worked hardest should get least. He repudiated the idea of compensation for landlords' (*OM*, 6 February 1884, 52).

Further questions followed, in a room whose acoustics seem to have been less than ideal; a brief moment of hilarity broke out when one speaker asking about the position of 'tenant farmers' was understood to be inquiring about the 'ten commandments' under socialism.

'Oxford went off well', Morris wrote cheerily in a letter to Thomas Cobden-Sanderson, and added: 'I wish you had been there and at Sydney Balls of St. John afterwards' (*CL*, II, 262). Sidney Ball, who had attended Hyndman's lecture and had clearly organised some kind of reception for the two speakers afterwards, was to become a well-known figure on the Oxford Left in the late nineteenth and early twentieth centuries, with G.D.H. Cole declaring him to be 'the recognised head of University Socialism' by 1908 (Ball, 228). Yet the exact nature of his politics remains elusive and it is not clear how close he would have been to Morris and Hyndman's revolutionary socialism in January 1884.

Born in 1857, Ball had at school 'played with great zest the forlorn role of red reformer', starting a magazine of Radical political sympathies, *The Rocket*, which was suppressed by the authorities after one issue (10); his great literary and political inspiration at this point in his life seems to have been Shelley's poetry. He went up to Oriel College, Oxford, in

1875, and after failing to get a First in Greats, studied philosophy in Germany for a time. In 1882 he was elected to a Lectureship in Philosophy and a Fellowship at St John's, at which time, a friend reported, he 'was trying ... to combine the organic view of the State which he had learnt from T.H. Green and from the German idealist philosophers, with the old individualist economics' (33–4). Socially aware undergraduates at St John's certainly saw the new arrival as part of the wider changes in Oxford that I sketched at the beginning of this chapter; Davey Biggs, who went up in autumn 1882, noted that 'of the new order of which we had been expectant, our new tutor was the embodiment' (205).

Ball was one of the original members and promoters of the Palmerston Club, an undergraduate Liberal organisation to the right of the Russell Club which had invited Morris to lecture in Oxford, and he did at least fifteen years' service to it as Senior Treasurer. In a letter to his wife-to-be in 1891 he very clearly declares himself 'as a Liberal', and notes that the President of St John's would welcome him as Proctor 'if I were not a Liberal' (49–50). On the other hand, Ball had joined the Fabian Society early in 1886 and played an important role in extending its influence at Oxford; as Janet Howarth puts it, 'from the early years of the Fabian Society Ball was its link with Oxford, inviting speakers to the Social Science Club in the 1880s' (*HUO*, VII, 2, 642). Yet even so, this may have been an identity he was not entirely happy with, for he wrote to his fiancée in 1891, 'I shall have to modify your account of me as a "Fabian"' (Ball, 55). After his death one St John's colleague described him as 'a strong Liberal ... with Socialistic views', another as 'essentially a Liberal. In many ways he was the successor of T.H. Green' (202, 224); and G.D. Cole noted wryly that the recognised Head of University Socialism found 'no difficulty in being at the same time President of the Oxford University Fabian Society and a leading member of the Liberal Club' (228). Ball had in fact confirmed such surmises in a letter of 1891: 'Do you know Arnold Toynbee's addresses? He was another of my "formative influences," but Green, I think, most of all' (241).

Sidney Ball's socialism, in short, was gradualist and reformist, far removed indeed from Morris's own revolutionary commitments in 1884. Yet Ball certainly had an admirable record of support for progressive causes at Oxford over the decades. Only three days after Morris's 1883

Oxford lecture, on 17 November, Ball held a meeting in his rooms at which the Reverend Samuel Barnett outlined a detailed plan for the university settlement in the East End of London which was to become Toynbee Hall, a project 'one day of which would be worth more than a hundred nights of our Utopian romancists', as the *Oxford and Cambridge Undergraduate's Journal* put it in a sideswipe at Morris (22 November 1883, III); at this meeting Michael Sadler was elected one of the two undergraduate secretaries. Toynbee Hall, in Barnett's words, would 'meet the sorrow and misery born of class division and indifference; it will bring classes into relation; it will lead them to know and learn of one another' (*HUO*, VII, 2, 671). Like the University Extension movement, it would do everything except abolish classes, which latter, in Morris's view, was the only aim politically worth pursuing.

Ball also put time and energy into Ruskin College, Barnett House and the Workers' Educational Association, but with his very moderate socialism, his tireless devotion to his college and his concern to strengthen the University as a centre for research and learning, he was never going to be the impassioned fighter who could have crucially supported Morris and Charles Faulkner in building a strong socialist organisation at Oxford. 'Few men in Oxford maintained so much contact with the militant thinkers of the day' (Ball, 210), so it does not surprise us to find him hosting Morris and Hyndman after their talk, but Ball was certainly not a militant man himself. 'You couldn't start the Class War with him', as one working-class admirer shrewdly put it, 'You might be a Socialist and wear whatever tie you like, but you buried class feeling in his presence' (248). Many years later, shortly before his death in May 1918, Sidney Ball made another brief appearance in the story of William Morris in Oxford, for 'one of the last things that he did in Oxford was to show Miss May Morris, at the Union, the photographs of the frescoes painted on its walls, so many years before, by her father and friends' (166–7).

The morning after the 1884 Clarendon Hotel meeting Hyndman and Morris went to the Bodleian Library – for what precise purpose we cannot be sure – when, to Hyndman's surprise, Morris was hijacked by the 'head librarian' and marched off to identify and catalogue a collection of illuminated medieval missals that the library had just purchased.

Surprise turned to astonishment as Hyndman watched Morris in action, and his account of the scene is a vignette justly popular with Morris biographers:

> So we went into an inner room, where a great pile of old illuminated missals lay upon the table. Morris seated himself by them, and, taking them up one by one, looked very quickly but very closely and carefully at each in turn, pushing it aside after inspection with 'Monastery So and So, date Such and Such,' 'Abbey this in such a year,' until he had finished the whole number; his decision being written down as he gave it. There seemed not to be the slightest doubt in the librarian's mind that Morris's judgement was correct and final. (Hyndman, 355)

We are familiar with Morris playing this kind of interactive role with the South Kensington Museum, which was always glad to draw on his professional expertise in relation to fabrics and carpets. And here we see in embryo a third, more interactive stage in his developing relationship with the city and University of Oxford. Morris in middle age is of course no longer the wide-eyed undergraduate that he had once been in the Bodleian, staring longingly at its cultural treasures and letting his own developing literary and artistic tastes be formatively shaped by them. But nor is he here either, as he had been just the evening before, the fire-breathing socialist revolutionary, keen to disperse the centralised treasures of elite institutions across the land, so that there would be a 'hundred British Museums instead of the one', as his interlocuter puts it in an interview of 1891 (Pinkney, 56). He is, rather, as he intently works his way through the pile of medieval missals, a co-worker or collaborator, neither passively taking from the University as in student days nor actively trying to refashion it altogether as in his activist mode, but rather interacting with it in shared cultural projects. We shall see more of Morris in this capacity in his dealings with Oxford in the last few years of his life, though such serener interchanges never drive out his activist anger entirely – far from it!

Morris had initially been briskly impatient at the very idea of getting caught up in the Bodleian's cataloguing operations: 'I have not come here to pore over missals. Besides I am with my friend and we have something else to do. I positively can't come' (Hyndman, 355). So who is this librarian who has enough persuasive power to morally twist Morris's arm into helping out, and who then accepts his judgements of date and place with such implicit confidence afterwards? Hyndman's 'head librarian' gives us the clue we need, for in 1882 Edward Nicholson, formerly librarian of the London Institution, had been appointed librarian of the Bodleian.

Nicholson and Morris had been acquainted for many years, since the former, then an undergraduate at Trinity College, Oxford, had written to Morris in November 1868 asking him to read and comment on a poem he had written. Morris duly obliged with a long critique on 3 December, finding the work derivative in relation to both contemporary and classical poetry, but none the less regarding it as 'quite good enough considering the circumstances' (*CL*, I, 72). Nicholson must have had an elastic spirit to bounce back from such faint praise, but he clearly did because six months later he again wrote to Morris, sketching out a series of literary ideas and projects. Morris replied from Bad Ems on 12 August 1869, approving of Nicholson's plans for editing an undergraduate literary magazine but offering some warning words based on his own experiences with the *Oxford and Cambridge Magazine* in 1856; he also challenged in some detail Nicholson's adverse remarks on Tennyson's poetry and shared thoughts with him over translations of the *Gesta Romanorum*. Both letters, thorough and detailed as they are, show Morris in an attractive light, taking seriously his responsibilities of nurturing undergraduate literary talent, and they alert us to an aspect of his relationship to Oxford which is not foregrounded in this study, devoted as it mainly is to architectural and political concerns. The Morris–Nicholson exchange of 1868–69 reminds us that Morris had a notable impact upon undergraduates as a poet, not just in later years as a SPAB or socialist activist. For as Andrew Lang, who arrived at Balliol from St Andrews in 1865, once remarked: 'I and several of my contemporaries at college knew the "Defence of Guenevere" almost by heart, before the name of Mr. Morris was renowned, and before he had published "The Life and Death of Jason"' (*CW*, I, xxij).

The acquaintance begun in these letters was sustained in later years, and became closer after Nicholson was appointed librarian at the London Institution in 1873 and proceeded with impressive energy to reactivate this almost moribund educational organisation. In 1877 he sent a copy of his *The Christ-Child and other Poems* to Morris and invited him to lecture at the Institution, an invitation the latter declined. In March 1880 Nicholson invited his mentor to attend Ruskin's lecture, 'A Caution to Snakes', at the Institution, and may have used the occasion to pile on the pressure to get a lecture out of Morris himself; for on 6 August we find Morris, 'with some misgivings', agree to deliver a talk on 'the Prospects of Architecture in Modern Civilisation', 'in the hopes that I shall have something to say' (*CL*, I, 577–8). His misgivings were clearly unfounded: he delivered the lecture successfully on 10 March 1881, and it was published as a strong concluding piece to *Hopes and Fears for Art* in 1882. Nicholson's enthusiasm for Morris's work certainly did not diminish, and in November 1881 the latter was having to fend off his admirer's invitation to become a regular contributor to some magazine in which he was involved. The last letter in the sequence of Morris's replies to Nicholson is dated 13 February 1882; in it he congratulates the latter on his appointment as Bodleian librarian. Nicholson had been appointed with support from Benjamin Jowett and with a brief to modernise the antiquated procedures of the Bodleian, which he proceeded to do with gusto in the teeth of entrenched opposition.

It was, then, this sixteen-year acquaintance which made the head librarian's request for help difficult to resist that January 1884 morning in the Bodleian, just as it was Nicholson's long-standing subaltern relationship to Morris that predisposed him to accept so unquestioningly Morris's attributions of date and place as he worked his way through the pile of illuminated missals. 'As you have made me your school-master I can't help it', Morris wrote in December 1868 (*CL*, I, 72–3), and in 1884 he was still to some extent playing this role to the younger man. It is true that no trace of Morris's socialism appears to have rubbed off on Nicholson, but the latter did play an energetic role in the anti-vivisection debates at Oxford in the 1880s (which led to Ruskin resigning his Slade Chair for a second time). Nicholson published *The Rights of an Animal: A New Essay on Ethics* in 1879, and in late 1883 the *Oxford and Cambridge Undergraduate's Journal* remarked that 'the anti-vivisectionists, championed to battle by the indefatigable Bodley's Librarian, are again coming to the fore' (1 November 1883, 45), so it appears that an activism of sorts had been communicated from mentor to pupil.

The Democratic Federation newspaper *Justice* had concluded its report on 'Mr. Hyndman at Oxford' (which does not mention Morris's presence at the event at all) with the confident claim that 'the seeds of Socialism have been sown in Oxford which will certainly bear good fruit' (16 February 1884, 7). But before this promising harvest could be reaped, before a new Oxford movement could be nurtured fully into being, the Democratic Federation – which had from August 1884 become the Social Democratic Federation (SDF) – had split disastrously asunder.

FOUR

The Socialist League at Oxford, 1885–88

I feel the job too heavy for myself alone: but Morris will come and help me.

Charles Faulkner, letter to J.L. Mahon, 22 January 1885 (*WMC*)

[N]aturally at Oxford no sincere revolutionist (using the word in its true sense) could escape hot water.

William Morris, letter to J.W. Brown, 10 March 1885 (*CL*, II, 402)

By the end of 1884 the brief-lived unity of purpose between William Morris and H.M. Hyndman was over. Disputes over Hyndman's political opportunism, his jingoism and his autocratic editing of the SDF newspaper, *Justice*, led to Morris and his allies walking out of the organisation in December 1884 and setting up the Socialist League, which from February 1885 had its own monthly newspaper, *Commonweal*. Morris's programme of lectures and speeches for 1885 is as prodigious as that for 1884, and it is striking how relatively important Oxford seems to be on the fledgling League's list of priorities. Morris's first speaking engagement outside London after the formation of the Socialist League was to Oxford, on 25 February, and he made three separate trips to speak in the city over the course of the year (the other two being in June and November), more than he made anywhere else, even to such major industrial centres as Manchester (two trips, in July and

September). Oxford was, of course, a good deal more convenient to get to than, say, Manchester or Glasgow, but even so it seems to count disproportionately in the League's first year of propaganda. Morris was determined, it would appear, to build on the momentum he had generated there as a Democratic Federation speaker in 1883–4; and if Oxford is indeed as structurally central to the distinctive socialism Morris was developing as I have suggested in my account of his 1883 lecture on 'Art under Plutocracy', then it clearly mattered to him to demonstrate this practically as well as theoretically, by establishing a thriving branch of the Socialist League in the city.

If Morris's aim was indeed to galvanise a 'new Oxford movement' into being through this series of speaking engagements in the city, then a model for what a successful student socialist movement might look like was afforded to him by Edinburgh University. It is true that Morris's assessment of Scottish undergraduate radicalism tended to waver. In July 1884 he wrote gloomily to Andreas Scheu that 'as to the students I fear that the damned religion is at the bottom of their hanging back' (*CL*, II, 300), but he felt able to give a more upbeat account to the *Daily News* interviewer in January 1885: 'He told me that he had found that ... Mr. Ruskin's influence is especially conspicuous in Edinburgh, where there is a Students' Socialist Society.' Morris declared that 'some of the most ardent Socialists are students of the University', but still felt the need to enter a caveat about the direction of undergraduate politics: 'They don't care anything about the merely political questions of Socialism – about legislative machinery and the like; what they do care for is the moral side of it, the introduction of a higher ethics into work and life' (Pinkney, 27–8). If there is a note of Marxist caution here about the fuzziness of student socialism, there is also, surely, admiration for the youthful idealism which broadens politics beyond the merely institutional into the wider reaches of everyday life and culture; it is, after all, in exactly that direction that Morris's own *News from Nowhere* so memorably heads.

The first issue of *Commonweal* in February 1885 contains an admiring report on the Edinburgh University Socialist Society, which had been formed by W.H. Campbell in the spring of the previous year. In the summer of 1884 its members had prepared and published a manifesto,

Beauty for Ashes: An Appeal, an impressively lucid statement of socialist principles which ends with the rousing words: 'Utopia now: we can bring it about. The power is ours if we have the will. This is surely an end to strive for. The work is ours, and yours, and, Students, it is worthy of you' (Edinburgh University Socialist Society, 15). The Society had organised a programme of visiting speakers, including Professor Beesly on 'Positivism versus Socialism' and W.R. Gorley on 'The New Socialism of the Chair', and had run weekly meetings at which such topics as French economics, Practical Socialism and the Credit system had been discussed. It had also opened a reading room containing a library of books on social questions, for the use of members and other reforming groups. Its membership was 'growing steadily' (*C*, February 1885, 3) and it thereby seems to offer a yardstick by which the success of socialism at other universities could be measured.

Could Morris and his fledgling Socialist League bring into being at Oxford a buoyant equivalent of the Edinburgh University Socialist Society, the nucleus perhaps of an entire new Oxford movement? In his attempt to do so, Morris had a crucial ally on the spot, Charles James Faulkner. I have already noted Faulkner's involvement in the 1883–4 Democratic Federation meetings in Oxford, but his involvement in the Socialist League was of a qualitatively different nature. On 1 February 1885 he wrote to its secretary, J.L. Mahon, that 'it makes me feel fresh again to be aiming at something in which I can feel an interest, after the miserable, dreary twaddle of university life' (E.P. Thompson, 390), and he donated one hundred pounds to the establishment of *Commonweal*. Such was his socialist passion from this point on that he even carried it with him on his vacations too, claiming to have converted the Norwegian captain and second mate of his ship on a trip to Sweden for health reasons that August, and he paid for copies of *Commonweal* to be sent out to Sweden through 1886, as if he were engaged on a one-man campaign to convert the country.

'Charley Faulkner, my inevitable travelling fellow': Morris's description of Faulkner, in a letter to Louisa Baldwin of March 1875, is true both literally and metaphorically (*CL*, I, 248). Faulkner was in northern France with Morris and Webb in summer 1858; he accompanied Morris on the two Iceland trips of 1871 and 1873, being his only English travelling companion on the latter expedition; the two men had a week's holiday together in Wales in April 1875, which is the trip Morris's colourful phrase to Louisa Baldwin refers to; and he was part of the first expedition up the Thames aboard *The Ark* in August 1881. But Charles Faulkner was part of Morris's life in a much more fundamental sense than this. He had been a central element of Morris's undergraduate life at Oxford. 'At Pembroke there was a little Birmingham colony', Burne-Jones later recalled, 'our common room was invariably Faulkner's, where about nine of the evening Morris and I would often stroll down together' from Exeter College (Mackail, I, 35–6). Faulkner's interests were mathematical and scientific rather than literary and artistic, but he certainly appreciated Morris's early intellectual distinction – 'How Morris seems to know things, doesn't he?' Faulkner once remarked to another contemporary, Richard Dixon (I, 44) – and there seems to have been a strongly physical side to their friendship which perhaps anticipates the later adventures together in Iceland; at any rate, Morris was 'fond of going down the river with Faulkner, who was a good boating man' (I, 43). As various biographers have noted, Morris's Birmingham undergraduate friends, with their experience of life in a major industrial city, may well have broadened his social horizons in these early years; Faulkner seems to have been well versed in topics such as sanitation and the Factory Acts and co-authored with Cormell Price an article on 'Unhealthy Employments' in the May 1856 issue of the *Oxford and Cambridge Magazine*.

Faulkner took two Firsts in mathematics and a First in natural sciences, and became a Fellow of University College in 1856 and a University Lecturer in mathematics in 1864. But despite his new professional commitments he remained close to the various artistic projects of his former undergraduate friends. This was easy enough when they took place in Oxford, and in the summer and autumn of 1857 he often popped across to the Oxford Union in the afternoons to help out with the decorative scheme or 'jovial campaign' progressing under Dante Gabriel Rossetti's generalship; 'Charley comes out tremendously strong on the roof with all kinds of quaint beasts and birds', Burne-Jones enthused in a letter home (Mackail, I, 120). And Faulkner was best man at Morris's wedding to Jane Burden in St Michael's Church, Oxford, on 26 April 1859.

The decamping of Burne-Jones and Morris to London in 1856 and the formation of their new decorative firm in early 1861 left Faulkner in a dilemma. But if it was a choice between Oxford and Morris, then Oxford, clearly, would have to go, and accordingly Faulkner resigned his mathematical tutorship and moved to London to study for a new career as a civil engineer and to keep the books for the Firm. The intimations of artistic ability which he had shown in the Oxford Union decorations were now developed further. He may have had no original gift for design, but his executive powers were impressive: he helped with mural decorations, painted pattern tiles and figure tiles, and reached the high point of his career as craftsman when 'in March, 1862, [he] success-fully cut a wood-block, on which Rossetti had drawn the well-known illustration for his sister's poem of "Goblin Market"' (Mackail, I, 146). Book-keeping was, however, clearly a waste of Faulkner's mathematical talents. He therefore returned to Oxford, in 1864, but since his mother and sisters had a house in Queen Square, where he spent much time during the vacations, he continued to play a significant role in the affairs of the Firm.

Faulkner, who seems to have been nicknamed 'The Fogger' at Oxford, was remembered by E.H. Hendon, an undergraduate from 1866 to 1870, as having a 'rather forlorn aspect' and as being mocked by the 'young bloods who used to jeer at his Birmingham boots'. After he became college bursar he did his best to revolutionise the aesthetic tastes of his undergraduate charges, but ended up 'complaining that the young Philistines used to take off Morris's lovely paperhangings' (Grylls, 199–200). There is a hint in these remarks that Faulkner was something of an outsider in his college even before he became a social-ist, and Morris himself described him in August 1867 as being 'now a don of University, though not much like one I must confess' (*CL*, I, 53). His role as bursar also involved him at the sharp edge of some of the urban processes that were so disturbing Morris about Oxford: new college building, for in the late 1870s he presided over the erection of a new Master's lodging at University College by Bodley and Garner; and suburban expansion, for the college owned land along the Banbury Road which developers in these years were very keen to get their profiteering hands on (Hinchcliffe, 56).

Having been drawn so deeply into Morris's craft and Icelandic enthusiasms, Faulkner, as the 'inevitable travelling fellow', was soon following him into politics too. 'I am very willing to receive you as a convert if you must needs ticket yourself so', Morris wrote to him in November 1876 in the run-up to the formation of the Eastern Question Association (CL, I, 330); and both he and Faulkner offered to help fund the new organisation. Faulkner travelled to London for the Workmen's Neutrality Demonstration in Exeter Hall in January 1878, and Morris was clearly confident that he could call on his support however hot the political temperature might become. In February he was writing to him about a planned demonstration in Hyde Park: 'there will certainly be a fight, so of course you will come up if you can' (CL, I, 444). When Morris switched his political allegiances from liberalism to socialism it was, therefore, virtually inevitable that Faulkner would do so too, though, as I noted above, he did not seem particularly active during 1883–84. But once the Socialist League broke away from the Democratic Federation he 'jumped in with both feet, set to work to organise an Oxford branch, and would have been ready to finish the job at once with dynamite if Morris had given the word' (E.P. Thompson, 322).

Faulkner's political writings during his socialist years are clearly not of the stature of Morris's, but at their best they are effective satirical or polemical interventions. His work in *Commonweal* ranges from brief reports of conversations with country folk during a walk around Marlborough to full-scale lectures on theoretical or political topics. 'Inhuman Arithmetic', serialised across three issues in July–August 1887, puts Faulkner's mathematical talents to good use in exposing the extreme disparities of wealth and poverty concealed beneath official economic statistics and their anodyne 'averages'. It is an effective satirical critique of the dehumanising assumptions of Political Economy in the spirit of John Ruskin's *Unto this Last*, and appropriately enough it quotes both Ruskin and Carlyle in its final paragraph.

'Law and War', serialised over four issues in January 1888, is a wide-ranging reflection on the functions of legal systems from Ancient Greece to contemporary rent strikes in Ireland. Its range of literary reference is as broad as its historical scope: Plato, Langland, Victor Hugo, Cobbett, Carlyle, Dickens and Leopold von Ranke all make appearances.

Faulkner's first conclusion, that all systems of law hitherto have been in effect acts of war of the possessing class against the dispossessed, is hardly surprising; but his second conclusion – 'the impossibility that any fixed legal system should continue even for a limited period to be in accord with reason and justice' – is more interesting (*C*, 21 January 1888, 29). For it points to a suspicion of law as such, not just of its prior historical manifestations, which may well point ultimately to anarchism rather than socialism. One would not say, on the basis of these and other articles, that Faulkner could ever emerge as a major theoretician of the nascent socialist movement; but they are certainly evidence of a highly capable, literate and committed mind, eminently suited both to leading the Oxford branch of the Socialist League and to mediating between it and the wider University community on the one hand and the national Socialist League organisation on the other.

On 20 February 1885 Morris wrote excitedly to his daughter May: 'Did you hear that Faulkner made his coup d'etat, and his radical association are turned Socialist Leaguers? Aveling and I are to go down to address them next Tuesday. Meantime F has got himself most heartily abused for his share in the proceedings chiefly, I believe for calling the deceased Burnaby "a scoundrel". The Telegraph even gave him the honour of an abusive leader: I suspect our friend is somewhat down-right in his oratory' (*CL*, II, 389). After one of Morris's legendary rages in the late 1850s Faulkner had stuck a label announcing 'He is mad' on his friend's hat before they went out; now, some twenty-five years later, as Morris's letter shows, both local and national newspapers were determined to stick just such a label on Faulkner himself. For as the *Oxford Review* opined, 'the hitherto somewhat obscure name of Faulkner has acquired considerable notoriety of late' (25 February 1885, 123).

The Oxford Radical Association had been formed in January 1885, but almost from the start there were attempts by socialists among its members to take it over; Faulkner once remarked mischievously that the chairman 'flattered me some time since by saying that he had never had an easy moment since I began to attend the meetings' (*WMC*, 10 January 1885). According to the *Oxford Chronicle and Berks and Bucks Gazette*, the Radical Association was on its last legs by the end of the month, with the socialist leaders Faulkner, Parker and Ogden pressing hard to take the organisation further to the left. At a meeting on 27 January Faulkner made one of the two remarks that became central to subsequent press coverage of Oxford socialism when he 'told those present that those who had gone into the questions that came within the sphere of Socialism were convinced that three hours work a day, if all worked, would be sufficient to maintain them in the same position as they then were' (*OC*, 31 January 1885, 6). There was much debate in the emergent socialist movement about what the ideal working day in a just society might be, and the Socialist League manifesto had argued that when labour was distributed fairly two to three hours daily work per person would be enough to produce the necessaries of life, leaving much time for intellectual and artistic pursuits (*J*, 6).

The internal turbulence within the Radical Association came to a head at the meeting of 3 February held in the Elm Tree Tavern, 95 Cowley Road (on the corner of what is now Jeune Street), where in the course of a ninety-minute speech Faulkner moved that 'the late Radical Association be changed into a Socialist Association'. We can hear occasional Morrisian inflections in Faulkner's speech, as when he declares that socialists 'wanted to enable those who were now ground down to lead a life in which there should be some element of beauty', but the remark that got taken up by the press occurs earlier in his long discourse. Arguing that socialism will lead to a higher conception of national duty, Faulkner asks: 'At present, what did patriotism mean? It meant that they should erect a statue to that murdering scoundrel Burnaby (Applause)' (*OC*, 7 February 1885, 6). Frederick Gustavus Burnaby had been a colourful adventurer and traveller as well as soldier. He had published accounts of his daring journeys on horseback through Asia Minor, and had successfully crossed the English Channel in a hot air balloon in 1882. As a colonel of the Horse Guards Blue, he had been killed on 17 January 1885, at the age of forty-two, in the battle of Abu Klea as a British force marched to the relief of General Gordon at Khartoum. Clearly, with Khartoum fallen and Gordon dead on 26 January, this was politically explosive territory for Faulkner to broach.

Faulkner's provocations, emanating from Oxford University of all places, were too much for the *Daily Telegraph* to swallow. It ran a brief piece on 'Oxford Communism' on 16 February, giving an account of

Faulkner's rhetoric that includes both the three-hour working day and the Burnaby references, and went on the attack in a sustained way on 17 February. 'When bad German philosophers die they go to Oxford', remarks the *Telegraph*, and Marx's influence has prompted Faulkner into 'something that is more like a shriek than a speech'. The reference to Burnaby as a scoundrel is deplored – 'even death does not disarm his [Faulkner's] criticism', remarks the leader writer – and the notion of a three-hour working day, as it is spelt out in more detail, ironically comes to seem more persuasive than the newspaper presumably wants it to be: 'At present artisans work on an average nine hours a day, but receive only a third of the profits resulting from their labour, the remaining two thirds going to the capitalists. When the workers take all ... there will be no necessity for working so hard.' However, gloats the newspaper, 'the stolid and unsusceptible character of the British work-man' will not let itself be taken in by 'wild rhetoric and irresponsible frivolity from obscure University Fellows' (*Daily Telegraph*, 17 February 1885, 5). Correspondents writing in over the next day or two, while sharing the paper's hostility to Faulkner's political views, felt that there was a danger in giving them so much prominence; for, as a self-declared 'Oxonian' announced, perhaps worried about the University's admissions figures, 'Those who are interested in Oxford, who have sons there, or sons who are going there, will be glad to learn that Mr. Faulkner is the solitary instance of a senior member of the University professing Anarchical opinions' (18 February 1885, 2).

The attacks continued in the local as well as national press. 'Just fancy it, sir; work for three hours a day, and yet live on the fat of the land!' wrote a correspondent to the *Oxford Chronicle* on 21 February. Faulkner himself had felt the sting of the press attacks sufficiently to defend himself in the same issue against the accusation of referring to Colonel Burnaby as a 'murdering scoundrel'. The *Chronicle*'s reporter had misrepresented his speech, he argues, which was not concerned to attack individuals who, from a Marxist viewpoint, are no more than 'mere helpless wheels in the terrible machinery of modern commerce' (*OC*, 21 February 1885, 8). All this publicity, clearly, could not but be beneficial in the run-up to the Morris–Aveling visit on Wednesday 25 February.

Was Faulkner putting himself at any professional risk by the political stance he was taking? We cannot be sure, but it is worth noting that the *Oxford Review* reported that 'some say he should be deprived of his fellowship; the *Pall Mall Gazette* thinks that steps should be taken against him' (18 February 1885, 110). Morris certainly realised that some academics were putting themselves at risk through their support for socialism. In his *Socialist Diary* he refers to the case of R.F. Muirhead, a lecturer in mathematics at Glasgow University who had chaired a socialist meeting: 'this really is courageous of him, considering his mildness and his position, as he is something at the University'; and Bruce Glasier commented in *Commonweal* in February 1887 that Muirhead and an academic colleague of his 'run seriously the risk of damaging their academic careers' (Boos, 33).

Advance publicity around Oxford for the lecture had been intense, with a political opponent complaining in the *Oxford Review* that 'our streets and shops have been placarded with Socialist "manifestos" and notices' (25 February 1885, 140–41). Morris himself was keen that there should be plenty of radical literature available on the night, asking John Mahon, the Socialist League secretary, if he had sent copies of the first issue of *Commonweal* down to Oxford in advance, and offering to take two quires down himself if not. But Faulkner had already been on the case, ordering 500 copies of *Commonweal* and the Socialist League manifesto to put on seats in the Holywell Music Room.

It had originally been intended to hold the talks in the Assembly Room of the Clarendon Hotel, but the proprietor, Mr Atwood, had become alarmed about possible disturbances and in the end refused to allow the meeting to take place there. It was therefore transferred to the Music Room in Holywell Street, which Morris described in a letter to Georgiana Burne-Jones as 'a room in Holywell, which I daresay you have forgotten: it used to be the room of the Architectural Society when I was a boy, and is now a music room: it is just opposite where Janey used to live – Lord, how old I am!' (*CL*, II, 392). The building had in fact been a concert hall long before it hosted the meetings of the Oxford Architectural Society in Morris's undergraduate days; and indeed Morris here seems to have forgotten that as students he and Edward Burne-Jones had belonged to the Plain-Song Society, which used to practise in the Holywell Music Room. It had been built between 1742 and 1748 as a dedicated concert hall and claims to be the oldest such building in Europe still in regular use. Haydn may have rehearsed there in 1791, and the building is best known today for its chamber music performances, especially the Sunday-morning Oxford Coffee Concerts which have been running since 1986. Situated at the east end of Holywell Street, the Music Room is just opposite St Helen's Passage, where Morris's wife-to-be, Jane Burden, had been born in an insanitary cottage in 1839. Her father, Robert Burden, worked as an ostler in Symonds' Livery Stable in Holywell Street itself. It seems apt enough, then, that Morris should have been lecturing on socialism here in February 1885, since this was the place which more than any other recalled his own great personal venture across the class divisions of Victorian society.

The organisers had made stringent efforts to control admission to the meeting, which was only granted on production of a ticket bearing the person's name; and on the evening itself there were supporters wearing red ribbons acting as stewards, and even, according to the *Oxford Chronicle*, several policemen ready to help maintain order. In that newspaper's view, 'there was a large audience, composed chiefly of undergraduates, and several ladies' (28 February 1885, 8); but Morris himself gave a politically shrewder assessment of the balance of forces in the Music Room in a letter to Georgiana Burne-Jones: 'you must understand that there were but some 20 or 30 of those enemies, and perhaps 100 declared friends, and some 250 indifferents who really came to listen to us: the hall was quite full' (*CL*, II, 393). Most of the enemies, in Faulkner's view, hailed from Merton College.

On the platform were Faulkner as chair, Morris and Aveling as speakers, and Eleanor Marx Aveling, Karl Marx's daughter and a leading socialist activist in her own right. The *Oxford Review* in a reflective piece on the meeting a week later gives us a vivid glimpse of the scene:

> Mr. Morris and Dr. Aveling present a strange contrast to one another. The poet is a bluff, honest-looking man; his forehead high, his face square set, and determined. With his long hair and grisly beard, he might well pass for an old sailor or fisherman. Dr. Aveling is a small, dark, clean shaven man, polite, almost oleaginous in manner. In a word, they rather reminded us of the lion and the fox. Mr. Faulkner,

melancholy, nervous, fidgety, was one of the worst chairmen we have
ever seen. (4 March 1885, 151)

Faulkner introduced the proceedings, accompanied, in Morris's
words, 'with only an average amount of howling' from hostile students,
and Morris himself then gave his 'first long speech without book': 'I
was rather nervous before I began … but the noise and life braced me
up, and after all I knew my subject, so I fired off my speech fairly well
I think' (*CL*, II, 392–3). The most detailed account of Morris's speech
is given in the *Oxford Chronicle and Berks and Bucks Gazette*, and I give
some significant excerpts from this in my thematic summary of the talk
so that the reader can judge what Morris was capable of at this point
in his speaking career in the way of extempore socialist rhetoric, and
can also, through the lively interjections and the speaker's responses to
them, get a more first-hand feel of this boisterous event. In contrast to
Aveling's speech, which tends towards the theoretical, Morris's is more
historical; whether this was a division of labour consciously decided
upon between them or simply the expression of their natural prefer-
ences, we cannot now know.

After Faulkner's brief introduction from the chair – itself the occasion
of 'great uproar' – Morris himself got under way:

> Mr. MORRIS, who was received with hisses and cheers in opening, said
> – Mr. Chairman, friends, and comrades ('Oh, oh.') In proceeding, he
> said that it seemed to him that a meeting of this sort, which was there
> to listen to some explanation of Socialism, had to deal particularly
> with four questions in the main; first of all, was the present condition
> of society under which they lived satisfactory? (Cries of 'Yes,' and
> 'No, no.') The second question was, what was the machinery which
> produced these conditions? The third was, could this machinery be
> altered? ('No.') Well, they were rather quick in answering; wait a little
> bit please. (Laughter and applause.) The fourth question was – and he
> dare say the greater part of them would think this the most important
> – in what direction could this machinery and the conditions of life that
> it produced be altered? (*OC*, 28 February 1885, 8)

Morris's quick retort to his heckler here clearly bears out his contention
in his subsequent letter to Georgiana Burne-Jones that 'the noise and life

braced me up ...they howled and stamped at certain catchwords, and our people cheered, so that it was very good fun' (*CL*, II, 393).

Answering his own first question, Morris denounces the material inequalities of contemporary society – inequalities which are not merely a moral matter of who has and has not the necessary thrift and capacity for hard work to rise socially, but which are systemic, destroying individuality and wasting talent at all social levels. But too many of the people who grasp the grievous problems caused by such inequalities also believe that the system is 'natural, necessary, and eternal', and it is in an attempt to dislodge their pessimism, to open them to prospects for transformation, that Morris embarks on his historical survey. Since there had been other modes of inequality in the past – based on race in the classical period, and on caste in the medieval period – then the capitalist inequality based on money was itself clearly just one more passing phase and would be superseded in its turn. 'These were the three sacred and holy words under which the people had always been oppressed – race, caste, and capital. (Great uproar.).'

The machinery which produces such inequality, Morris continues, is the extraction of unpaid labour from the working population by the non-producing class. Can such machinery be changed, he asks, moving on to his third question? The French Revolution had shown that wholesale change was possible and England too had been in serious turmoil: '"For about 15 years," said a foreigner, "England was in a state of chronic insurrection." (Loud cries of "No, no.") Some gentlemen who made so much noise had perhaps not read the history of Chartism. (Hear, hear, and laughter.) When they read that, if they did so with sufficient attention, they would understand a few things that they did not understand now ("Oh, oh," and uproar.).' True, the class struggle had then settled down into a period of trade-union reformism, labour aristocracy and commercial prosperity, but now, with England losing its dominant position in the world economic system, class struggle was sharpening again.

What the working class therefore aims at, argues Morris, picking up his fourth question about the direction of social change, is the common ownership of the means of production and exchange; and he moves on to a vivid evocation of what such a fully socialised economy and culture

would look like, though, as we should expect, this was hardly enough
to stop the hecklers:

> The quiet improvement of men's faculties, the progress of knowledge,
> new birth of art, life no more a blind hurrying stumble from the cradle
> to the grave ... The State would no longer sacrifice even one man to
> the common good; they would live for themselves, and each other and
> the community, which they would feel to be themselves; it would be
> a case of all for each as well as each for all. (A voice: 'Come along, oh
> happy day!' and laughter).

Not that the hecklers had everything their own way: one undergraduate
complained that when he had tried to object to one of Morris's claims
he had been violently hit over the head by a steward.

The *Oxford Review* found Morris's talk to be 'rather rough and unpolished, even choleric in tone, but it bore the impress of sincerity and
attained to a rude eloquence in places'. But it regarded Edward Aveling
as in another class altogether: 'Dr. Aveling is a really fine speaker. Impassioned, plausible, seductive, and saponaceous in turn, he so tickled
his audience's taste, and patted them on the back that it was not until
he had sat down that they realised the audacity of his opinions.' This
was high praise from the newly founded review of the conservative
Non-Placet Society, though true to its political roots it then went on to
conclude that both Morris and Aveling 'showed considerable ignorance
of history and political economy' (4 March 1885, 151).

In the early months of 1885 Aveling was giving a set of lectures on
Marx's *Capital* at the South Place Institute in London, and he comes
before his Oxford audience as the Marxist theorist concerned to stress
the scientific basis of socialism – 'What Darwin had done for biologi-
cal science, they believed that Marx and his school had done for economical science' – and to expound the difference between use-value and
exchange-value (*OC*, 8). However, the theoretical cast of his discourse
did not prevent him from making some sharp local polemical points.
Expounding the basis of profit in unpaid labour, he suddenly turned
upon Oxford University, asking 'Where did all the emoluments of every
college in Oxford come from?' The task of socialists, as Aveling here sees
it, is education towards the abolition of private ownership of the means
of production, and he concluded his talk by looking forward to a time

when the 'magnificent buildings' among which he was lecturing would belong to the people as a whole.

After the two talks Faulkner as chair invited questions, and enquiries about the origins of capital and the socialist concept of equality were directed to the two speakers. The liveliest moment came, however, when a venturesome undergraduate asked permission to pose a 'somewhat personal question' to Morris; Faulkner demurred, but Morris insisted on taking it, at which point an objection he would have to face over and over was put forward: 'whether Mr. Morris divided the profits of his business among his workmen or distributed it over the country'. Morris's reply, to the effect that he did all he could for his workmen but could not take himself out of the present condition of society, did not satisfy the student, who retorted: 'how do you mean to bring your principles into general favour, if you, being the leader of that movement, refuse to give up your capital?' (*OC*, 8).

Morris seems to have regarded the question about himself as capitalist as a fair part of the evening's political rough and tumble. But official Oxford was not amused by it, with the *Oxford Magazine* loftily remarking: 'We could wish that personalities had been kept out of the discussion. It was scarcely in good taste to question Mr. Morris about the conduct of his business' (4 March 1885, 122). Other organs sided more with the student, finding Morris's reply as being 'of an evasive character' (*JOJ*, 28 February 1885, 8).

The meeting ended colourfully enough, though not quite as colourfully as Arthur Stringer suggests when he recalls 'that winter day in Holywell, in 1885, when the undergraduates of his *alma mater* derisively pelted [Morris] with eggs and old vegetables, transforming an orderly meeting into open riot' (Stringer, 127). What in fact happened was that, as the *Cambridge Review* wryly put it, 'Mr. W. Morris and Dr. Aveling were refuted by the invincible logic of rowdyism and stinking chemicals' (4 March 1885, 249). Stephen Gwynne, who was in the audience as a student, gives a view of proceedings from the floor: 'Some youthful High Tory ... provided himself with a large bottle of sulphuretted hydrogen, which he opened surreptitiously at the back of the room. The effect was instantaneous. I remember the astonished faces of the people on the platform; till, as the wave of pocket-handkerchiefs spread towards them, they gradually discovered the grim fact' (Gwynne, 42). In fact, the political opposition seems to have dominated the last, disorderly moments of the meeting. One hostile undergraduate stood on a seat and proposed a motion that the meeting did not agree with the views expressed by the speakers, which was carried 'by a large majority of those remaining', and the National Anthem was sung 'with great heartiness' (*OC*, 8).

After the lecture Morris, Faulkner and the Avelings retired to dine at Morris's hotel with some of the undergraduates. Also of the party, at Morris's invitation, was Ingram Bywater, who had even, in a strange misjudgement of his politics, been invited to sit on the platform with the speakers earlier in the evening (he declined). As Bywater left the room 'he remarked to a friend that he now understood the elements which contributed to the making of a revolution. There was the man who had a quarrel with society, the honest enthusiast, and the interested and intriguing adventurer' (W. Jackson, 42–3). This, which constitutes the first recorded comment on the evening, presumably assigns Morris to the role of enthusiast, Aveling (of whose tarnished sexual and financial reputation in the socialist movement Bywater may have had some prior knowledge) as the adventurer, and Faulkner, somewhat mysteriously, as the man with the grudge. The undergraduates later conducted Morris and his party to the New College cloisters 'to see their loveliness under the moon' (*CL*, II, 393) – an appropriate choice, given that 'this was the corner of old Oxford Morris loved the most' (MacCarthy, 516).

It wasn't only the socialist students who were busy that night in the wake of the lecture, as Morris noted with amusement in a letter to his daughter May a fortnight later: 'the organized opposition [at the lecture] quite failed; so much so that in dudjeon [*sic*] against the incapacity of their leader the malcontents broke his windows that same night; a frankness quite charming. Still some of the young gentlemen were very rude, especially to Faulkner. They have a donkey-race on this week or last, and have dubbed one of the donkeys "Socialist" and another "Comrade Faulkner"' (*CL*, II, 402–3).

Morris and Aveling's talk at the Holywell Music Room had not been the only public event devoted to socialism in Oxford that week in February. There had also been a meeting under the auspices of the Guild of St Matthew at which Henry Cary Shuttleworth had expounded the principles of Christian Socialism, though, as the *Cambridge Review* noted, 'the Christianity predominated over the Socialism' (4 March 1885, 249). Shuttleworth, who lectured on pastoral and liturgical theology at King's College, London, was president of the Oxford branch of the Guild of St Matthew, which had been formed by F.L. Donaldson at Merton College in 1884. Such socially concerned Christian organisations were springing up at a great rate from the late 1870s: the Guild itself had been founded by Stewart Headlam in 1877; the monthly journal *Christian Socialist* first appeared in June 1883; the Christian Socialist Society was set up in London in 1886, followed by the Christian Social Union in 1889. Peter Jones has demonstrated in an extensive study of the movement just how many of its leading figures Oxford produced: in the 1870s, Shuttleworth himself and W.E. Moll for the Guild of St Matthew, and Henry Scott Holland, J.R. Illingworth and Charles Gore for the Christian Social Union; in the 1880s, James Adderley and Percy Dearmer for the Church Socialist League. There was even a Reverend W. Morris (Guild of St Matthew), who had graduated from New College in 1880, became a curate in Vauxhall, and whose workers' club there was 'a planning center for labor demonstrations and the headquarters of the great London gas strike, which Morris helped to lead' (Jones, 245).

William Morris and Charles Faulkner subsequently exchanged thoughts about Henry Shuttleworth by letter. Morris dismisses his notion of 'Socialism by taxation', regarding it as no less half-hearted than the Positivist doctrine of the 'Moralization of Capital', while Faulkner wonders whether he ought to have a stab at converting Shuttleworth to the full-blooded revolutionary creed. Though Morris himself devoted much epistolary time and energy to converting Christian Socialists (or trying to), he thinks the effort to win over Shuttleworth, with his tepid blend of 'compromise plus sentiment', is unlikely to be worthwhile and concludes that 'one lecture of his against one of ours might have made him seem nearer to us than he is' (*CL*, II, 400). We have no record of whether Faulkner did try to convert Henry Shuttleworth, and to do so would clearly have been quite a challenge, given Peter Jones's vivid evocation of the man: 'He was the ideal type, the perfect exemplar, of the jolly, back-slapping, high-living, broad-minded, liberal athletic Anglican parson so often caricatured in fiction and film, of which Charles Kingsley was the early mode' (Jones, 118). But it was clear, more generally, that Christian Socialism at Oxford was not going to go away, and, as we shall see, it did in fact comfortably outlast both the local branch of the Socialist League and its undergraduate spin-off, the Marx Club.

Marx and Aveling had certainly galvanised some members of their Oxford audience to extend their political education, for the former noted that 'two or 3 of our Oxford friends' attended the commemoration of the Paris Commune organised in London by the Socialist League and various anarchist groups on 22 March (*CL*, II, 407).

Morris returned to Oxford on 9 June 1885, the day Gladstone's government resigned, to lecture to a joint meeting of the Oxford branch of the Socialist League and the Marx Club. On 9 February Faulkner had written optimistically to J.L. Mahon that the Oxford branch was 'gradually getting known among undergraduates. There were half a dozen present tonight including G. Brown, who is a delightful and most sensible young fellow' (*WMC*, 9 February 1885), but this unity between students and workers does not seem to have lasted long. For a separate Marx Club, according to the pamphlet *Red Oxford*, was 'the first undergraduate socialist body' and thus a left-wing equivalent of the Palmerston and Russell Clubs, and may have survived till 1892 (Ashley and Saunders, 6). How much it actually knew of Marx's work, however, is a moot point. Morris and Faulkner discussed the Marx Club in an exchange of letters, with the former doubting that a university socialist group could last, given the inevitable annual turnover of undergraduates; 'still if they won't come into the movement any other way, that way might be tried' (*CL*, II, 399)

Mainstream scholarly tradition has it that Morris's second 1885 Oxford lecture was titled 'Socialism'; this tradition begins with May Morris and is followed by those meticulous Morris scholars Eugene LeMire and Nicholas Salmon. Let us assume for the moment that this is so. May Morris, handling a tattered manuscript 'worn to rags and eloquent of many journeyings', described this text as belonging to a category of 'elementary explanations of the beliefs of the party, partly intended for those outside the movement, and partly for our own people who were themselves new to the various points they would have to teach'; so to this extent it might seem apt enough as a lecture to an undergraduate audience. Morris considered the text successful enough to deliver it no less than twelve times, according to LeMire – the Oxford event in his view being the first in this sequence. The manuscript is in some respects a palimpsest of these travels, as May Morris notes: 'On the verso of several pages at the end are notes of points in discussion, made in an exquisite hand with a finely pointed pencil; and some delightful decoration – one a flower-border of our Thames-side fritillary, so crisp and dainty!' (*AWS*, II, 192).

This last quaint detail reminds us that if we are going to do a thorough accounting of Morris's debt to Oxford, we shall have to include not only its architecture, illuminated manuscripts and intellectual influences, but also its natural environment. For as Arthur Stringer aptly points out:

> It was the Oxford fritillary, that little, checkered, purplish flower commonly called the snake's-head, which blooms so beautifully along the Isis, about Iffley, in the late spring, which gave to William Morris one of his favourite flower designs. The slender spike of the Oxford wild-tulip, which you will to-day find flowering about the meadows of the Cherwell, furnished him with an equally happy design. (Stringer, 130)

Any full accounting of Morris's feelings about the Oxford countryside would also have to include Godstow, of which he wrote in the summer of 1882 that it was 'less changed than any beautiful place I know, the very fields that stretch up to Wytham the same as they always were with their wealth of poplar and willow trees, the most beautiful meadows to be seen anywhere' (*CL*, II, 123).

But the detailed *Commonweal* report to the 1885 annual general meeting of the Socialist League does not accord with the views of May Morris, LeMire and Salmon. It reads in part as follows: 'On Monday June 9, William Morris and L. Gronlund lectured to a meeting of about 80, organized by the Oxford branch and the Marx Club acting together. The subjects of the lectures were "Useful Work v. Useless Toil" and "Socialism as a Necessary Development of Society"' (*C*, Supplement to August, 73). By this point, according to the report, the Oxford branch, perhaps inspired by the Edinburgh University Socialist Society, had founded a library of about sixty volumes, mostly on socialist topics but with some general literature interspersed among the heavier tomes. Faulkner, as librarian, had been greatly exercised in the purchase of the books, knowing that they could all too easily be far above the heads of the branch's working-class members.

So it was, after all, 'Useful Work versus Useless Toil' which Morris delivered on his second 1885 visit to Oxford. This was one of his most popular and often repeated lectures, and, in its vision of a society that has overcome the division between intellectual and manual labour, seems well attuned to bridge the social divide in his audience between the working-class members of the Socialist League and the student members of the Marx Club. Moreover, the lecture is a powerful statement of a distinctively Morrisian Marxism. It reiterates some basic expository aspects of his first 1885 Oxford lecture, but then moves decisively beyond this, into questions of popular art or pleasure in labour, thereby picking up some of the profounder themes of the November 1883 lecture in University College hall.

Morris begins by setting out, in the abstract, what in his view distinguishes useful work from useless toil and comes up with a threefold scheme: it is 'hope of rest, hope of product, hope of pleasure in the work itself' which gives us 'a pair of scales in which to weigh the work now done in the world' (*CW*, XXIII, 99–100). He then offers a panoptic survey of work (or the lack of it) in contemporary society. The aristocracy consumes prodigiously but produces nothing; the middle class appears to work hard, but in fact actually produces nothing; all labour is backbreakingly imposed upon the working classes. And much of the work that is actually done is wasted, in the excessive advertising of wares, or the production of pointless and degrading luxuries for the upper classes or of cheap and sham necessities for the lower classes. If, therefore, the socialist revolution abolishes the classes that live off other people's labour, putting them back to work, and also redirects social labour power to genuinely worthwhile production, then the worker will have the full benefit of what he or she produced (rather than having it drained away in the form of surplus value) and the working day will consequently be radically shortened. Hence two of Morris's criteria for useful labour – hope of rest and hope of product – would be abundantly satisfied, and the lecture has thus spelt out the intellectual background to that provocative claim of Faulkner's for a three-hour working day which aroused so much derision in the local and national press earlier in the year.

'Some Socialists might say we need not go any further than this', Morris continues (107); but his third criterion, hope of pleasure in the work itself, has not yet been met. If work were indeed equitably shared across society and devoted only to genuinely useful production, then this would be a vast improvement on the injustice and waste of capitalism itself, but such work would still be a daily burden on humanity, albeit a greatly reduced and justly distributed one. 'We may hope that men who have just waded through a period of strife and revolution will be the last to put up long with a life of mere utilitarianism, though Socialists are sometimes accused by ignorant persons of aiming at such a life' (III). The next stage, then, is to get pleasure or creativity into the labour process, so that it becomes not just a mechanical chore but an aesthetic delight too.

Some socialists, Morris notes, may find his suggestions under this heading 'strange and venturesome'. These controversial issues include, crucially, the notion of 'variety of work', and it is here, one speculates, that he might have made most impact on his Oxford audience. For he sketches out a holistic model of labour that, if instituted, would transform the lives of both the students and the workers who were listening to him:

> To compel a man to do day after day the same task, without any hope
> of escape or change, means nothing short of turning his life into a
> prison-torment. Nothing but the tyranny of profit-grinding makes this
> necessary. A man might easily learn and practice at least three crafts,
> varying sedentary occupation with outdoor – occupation calling for the
> exercise of strong bodily energy for work in which the mind had more
> to do. There are few men, for instance, who would not wish to spend
> part of their lives in the most necessary and pleasantest of all work
> – cultivating the earth. (112)

One wonders what the undergraduates in the room made of this last assertion, though there is clearly a distant echo in this passage generally of John Ruskin's road-building scheme of 1874 to which, as we shall see later, Morris reverts again in *News from Nowhere*.

It is only a transformed education system, Morris continues, which can secure such radical ends: education must become a holistic process of eliciting the full range of young people's talents rather than the commercial treadmill it is at present, for 'even at the ancient universities learning is but little regarded, unless it can in the long run be made *to pay*' (113). Once variety of work has been achieved under socialism, then creativity can be reintroduced into the labour process, as Morris reverts strongly to the themes of his great 1883 Oxford address: 'I mean that side of art which is, or ought to be, done by the ordinary workman while he is about his ordinary work, and which has got to be called, very properly, Popular Art' (113).

'Useful Work versus Useless Toil' thus finely serves the twin aims of giving a basic exposition of socialist demands in relation to work along with a stirring vision of Morris's own distinctive further demands in this area. The socialist utilitarians may win out in the first instance, but pleasure and creativity in labour remain the decisive long-term goal, and 'we will accept the passing phase of utilitarianism as a foundation for the art which is to be' (116). The talk carefully repeats some of the basic points that Morris had made to his Oxford audience in February, but then stretches their imaginations in directions that even some of his own senior Socialist League colleagues in London might not have been prepared to take.

Morris's 9 June Oxford audience enjoyed a real feast of socialism that day, for they had before them not one but two important figures in the international movement. Morris's co-speaker, Laurence Gronlund, a Danish American, played an important role in the American Socialist Labor Party and had just published *The Cooperative Commonwealth in its Outlines* (1884), which presented a concise account of German socialism to an English-speaking audience, and which Morris described in May 1885 as 'modest & accurate in tone, and has a good deal of information in it' (*CL*, II, 431). In an article on 'The Work Before Us' in the July 1885 issue of *Commonweal*, Gronlund confirms his recent presence in Oxford and gives us some sense of the content of his talk: 'As the writer of this the other day told the students at Oxford, the grand doctrine of Evolution which English scientists have installed on the throne of the human mind is the greatest intellectual revolutionary development since Copernicus, since it is nothing less than the divine basis on which the splendid edifice of Socialism is to be reared' (*C*, 1 July 1885, 62). During

Gronlund's stay in Europe from 1885 to 1887 he 'seemed to cast a spell over the editors of the *Christian Socialist*', and 'the phrase "cooperative commonwealth" recurs in [Christian Socialist] rhetoric throughout the 1890's' (Jones, 324). For the Socialist League to have used Gronlund as a speaker in Oxford may thus have been a deliberate ploy to appeal to the undergraduate religious left in the wake of Morris and Faulkner's discussion of Henry Cary Shuttleworth's lecture in February.

Back in London, meantime, the pace of political events was hotting up. The police attacks on socialist meetings there which had begun in May 1885 gathered intensity across the summer and on 21 September, at the trial of various comrades for 'obstruction' at Dod Street the previous day, Morris himself was in the dock before Judge Thomas Saunders for supposedly assaulting a policeman. Yet despite the urgent pressures of the Free Speech campaign of these months, senior figures of the Socialist League still found time to visit Oxford. In early October Andreas Scheu, Viennese socialist, furniture designer and one of Morris's key allies in the League, was in the city, though whether this was a political mission or just a holiday we cannot now establish (*CL*, II, 467).

There was no let-up in the vigour of Oxford socialism as the year approached its end. Morris reported to a Socialist League general meeting which he was too unwell to attend that

> Faulkner has invited me to lecture for the oxford Branch [*sic*] on Tuesday 10th Nov: & also to address an undergraduate club on 13th & that I have accepted both invitations. In case Faulkner has not written to the League I note as a matter that will interest you that the Oxford Branch held a meeting at Wheatley a village near oxford [*sic*] last Saturday which was attended by over 100 agricultural labourers, who were much interested. (*CL*, II, 481)

We thus find the Oxford branch responding at last to C.W. Mowbray's appeal in an early issue of *Commonweal*: 'Comrades, – Our time has arrived for earnest out-door propaganda' (*C*, June 1885, 47); I have, though, found no evidence that they ever conducted outdoor meetings in Oxford itself. To Faulkner himself Morris wrote: 'I am very glad to hear about the success of your Wheatley meeting; it would be a very good deed to spread the light among the country people' (*CL*, II, 482). He had some hopes of doing so himself, since he was negotiating with Oswald Birchall, the rector at Buscot, a village near Kelmscott, about addressing the field labourers there later in November in order to demonstrate to them 'the evils of party government' in the run-up to the 1885 general election (*CL*, II, 484). Morris's continuing ill health meant that this proposed talk did not in the event materialise, and it was not until December 1887 that he lectured at Buscot on 'Socialism and the London Disturbances'.

Morris travelled to Oxford on Tuesday, 10 November 1885, just after drafting the Socialist League 'Don't Vote' manifesto for the general election, and his third and last Socialist League lecture at Oxford took place that evening in the Holywell Music Room, with Faulkner in the chair. Morris had been suffering so badly from gout that autumn that his daughter May travelled with him to Oxford. 'I go', she wrote wryly to George Bernard Shaw, 'to "take care of him"'. Taking care of him is a real farce: I give him wonderfully sage advice to his health which I need not say he does not follow' (MacCarthy, 530). Morris's gout was in fact so painful that he had to lecture sitting down rather than standing. He reported afterwards to his other daughter Jenny that 'the meeting at Oxford went off very well last night: the place was crowded, & generally sympathetic; & although there were some dozen or so of Tory young gentlemen, they behaved themselves fairly well'. He had, however, paid a price in terms of health for this trip: 'I have been to oxford [*sic*] and am back & perhaps I had better not have gone ... I keep on being lame in my left foot, & cant shake it off – the lameness I mean, my dear, not the foot' (*CL*, II, 489). It seems likely that on account of Morris's continuing health problems the second lecture planned on this expedition, to the Eglesfield Club at Queen's College, did not take place, though I shall say something about the 'concept' of that lecture at least below.

Morris's third lecture in the Holywell Music Room certainly elicited less press interest than his first one of the year, as we might expect in the run-up to the first general election under the new Reform Act; but a report in the *Oxford Magazine* gives us some sense of the scene, with 'the self-selected four hundred "with a genuine interest in Socialism"' forming an ample audience, who were treated to 'the Lecturer's usual charm of diction, and their own unusual harmony' (18 November 1885, 388). But this relative lack of press coverage certainly does not reflect any lack of merit in the lecture itself. Morris had written to Faulkner on 2 November that 'I must ask you to put up with the [lecture] I delivered at the Working-Mans College under the name of "Socialism"' (*CL*, II, 482), a remark which may possibly have contributed to May Morris's error over the topic of his second 1885 Oxford lecture; but he had clearly changed his mind between writing this letter and the actual visit. For the lecture given was in fact 'The Rise of a New Epoch'; it was delivered for the first time on this Oxford trip, was then given five more times during 1886, and finally, retitled as 'The Dawn of a New Epoch', it became the concluding piece in the 1888 collection *Signs of Change*.

The lecture begins, as one would expect from its title, with a rousing evocation of changing historical epochs, in which the seeds of the new gain strength and burst through an old, decaying order. 'We are now living in one of these times of conscious change', Morris asserts (*CW*, XXIII, 122); but the battle is not now between Absolutism and Democracy – an issue basically settled by the French Revolution of 1789 – but between Mastership and Fellowship. His hope is that the latter 'will develop naturally, and probably with no violent conflict' (123).

The bulk of the lecture comprises a detailed and lucid exposition of how the possessing class extracts surplus value from the labour of the working class through its monopoly of the means of production; and Morris announces that such surplus value 'is no trifle, but amounts to at least two-thirds of all that the worker produces' when taxes, rent and commission to middlemen are taken into account (129). He thus again implicitly agrees with that remark of Charles Faulkner's which had sparked off so much press controversy and ridicule at the start of this year that a mere three-hour working day would be necessary in a socialist society that had expropriated the expropriators.

Morris does not descend into the specifics of how the socialist organisation of labour would be enacted, but reflects on some more general issues which he knows are likely to come up otherwise as questions at the end of his talk. 'You will no doubt want to know what is to become of private property under such a system' (134), just as his audience is 'sure to want an exposition of the Socialist views here as to those who direct labour or who have specially excellent faculties towards production' (136). He concludes with a vision of the centralised nation-state withering away into the 'Federation of Independent Communities'. In the early stages of socialism 'some kind of centre' would still be necessary to safeguard the principle of association rather than competition, but in the fully developed socialist society, which Morris would rather call communism, 'those principles would be recognized by everyone always and intuitively, when the last vestiges of centralization would have died out' (139–40), which is the very stage Morris will a few years later be concerned to dramatise in *News from Nowhere*.

There were questions at the end of Morris's lecture, 'mostly on matters of detail', according to the *Oxford Magazine*. The dozen Tory young gentlemen seem to have given him the usual ribbing over being himself an employer of labour, and then really hit below the belt by mocking the fact that he, as a socialist, suffered from gout, which they described as 'the aristocratic tyrant' – a jibe which the *Oxford Magazine* magisterially described as 'malicious but … not dialectically effective' (18 November 1885, 374). But, as its reporter noted, 'perhaps the most interesting answer elicited was, that "about 20 years" should be necessary for the fulfilment of [the] prophecies' in the main body of the talk (*OM*, 388). It is certainly the case more generally that in his letters of late 1885 Morris is optimistic about major social change coming relatively soon, despite the severity of police attacks on socialist meetings during those months.

As I have noted, it is likely that Morris's second scheduled Oxford talk that week, to the undergraduate Eglesfield Club of Queen's College, did not actually take place due to his problems with gout. But we do have its title, 'Socialism: the True Road to Individual Development', and the resolution around which it was to be based:

> That the system of Society which is founded on the division of mankind into classes, governing & governed, rich & poor, producing & non-producing, accompanied as it necessarily must be by competition for position & existence throughout all classes, is now proving itself wasteful, obstructive to progress, is becoming effete, and must give place to a system which while recognizing the varied capacities of men will ensure equality of condition for all. (*CL*, II, 482)

It is in the emphasis on the varied capacities of men here that the intriguing potential of the title is indicated.

Morris had floated the notion of individual development in his first 1885 talk at Oxford when he argued that, given the gross inequities of contemporary society, 'a man born to this inequality had his capacity made nothing of, and he was pressed down into the mire, and his individuality was destroyed' (*OC*, 28 February 1885, 8). May Morris notes tartly how regularly the issue used to come up in questions after socialist lectures: 'In discussion-time at Socialist meetings then and thereafter one of the stock objections of the Regular Opponent was that individuality would be lost in a Socialist Society, the Objector himself, so anxious on this score, being usually a fine example of machine-made mentality' (*AWS*, II, 107). It is tempting to think, on the basis of Morris's proposed title, that he intended to give the theme of individualism a specifically Oxford inflection and address that local form of it known as Aestheticism, first formulated in the Conclusion to Walter Pater's *Studies in the History of the Renaissance* (1873) and given new currency by Oscar Wilde's flamboyant undergraduate career at Oxford between 1875 and 1878. We have noted above Arthur Quiller-Couch's contention that Aestheticism was waning in Oxford in the early 1880s, but there was still some of it about there in these years, with aesthetically minded students declaring that riding on top of the new Magdalen Bridge trams was the only exercise they ever took. But with no surviving text for Morris's Eglesfield Club lecture we have no real warrant for thinking it might have tackled Paterian and Wildean definitions of individual development amidst the dreaming spires that were their very homeland. The non-existent lecture can thus remain as fertile a field for the critic's imagination as the apocryphal but oft-mentioned visit of Oscar Wilde to Morris on the latter's deathbed in 1896.

By the end of 1885 and after Morris's three visits to rouse the troops, the Oxford branch of the Socialist League had a modest total of about twenty-four members, although an Oxford report to the League's London office declares confidently: 'Have every reason to believe that all members are good ones' (*WMC*, undated, possibly early 1886). Faulkner remarks that 'all the members except myself are working men' (19 November 1885), and we do get occasional brief glimpses of some of them in the course of his correspondence with the League's central office. There is an elderly and direly impoverished German, Guggenheim, the 'most intelligent member' (30 January 1885), who offers to translate pieces from the foreign press and to get them into local Oxford newspapers; there is the secretary, A.S. Robinson, 'not dishonest, but ... one of those sloppy characters on which no reliance is to be placed' (26 May 1885); there are the workmen from Mr Harris's Cricket Ball manufactory in the Iffley Road, who may well have been putting their jobs on the line in attending socialist meetings; and there is G. Brown, the exception that proves the rule about the membership, since he is the only University man who sticks to the Socialist League rather than peeling off into the Marx Club.

Faulkner's assessment of the branch and of his own capacity for political leadership of it vary widely. We have noted his jubilant sense of a new direction after the dreary twaddle of university life, but, as my epigraph to this chapter suggests, there was a darker side to his involvement too. On a good day he could announce, 'I am happy to say that we are already subject to persecution' (*WMC*, 1 February 1885), but there were also gloomier moments, as when he wrote to J.L. Mahon that 'I confess I am disheartened' as the university men flaked away and formed the Marx Club: 'It is too great a burden on me to frame a lecture worth listening to once a week ... The other and standing difficulty which so oppresses me is to find something for the members of the Branch to do. I feel puzzled and ill & unfit for post' (29 April 1885). Part of Faulkner's difficulty here surely lay in the very nature of the Socialist League's political 'purism', which forbade it to contest parliamentary elections or get involved in anything it regarded as palliative measures – at which point all that was left was a programme of lectures and selling *Commonweal*. But part of the problem also resided in the capacities, or lack of them, of the group itself; for as Faulkner complains: 'it is so very difficult to create a feeling of responsibility in the various members of the Branch' (1 June 1885).

We can track the progress of the Oxford branch of the Socialist League through Faulkner's letters back to the London centre and through reports appearing in *Commonweal*. Early in 1886 we learn that 'Oxford has held its meeting weekly and has given two public lectures which have been fairly well attended, viz, on November 30th [1885], "Socialist Experiments in America", on December 9, "The Theory of Population in regard to Socialism"' (*C*, January 1886, 8). The weekly meetings at this point take place at 8.30 p.m. on Mondays in the Elm Tree Tavern on the Cowley Road, but the venue changes from April 1886 to the Temperance Hall, 27 Pembroke Street.

The branch had by now persuaded two local newsagents to sell *Commonweal* – Mr English, 38 St Ebbes Street, and Mrs Foy, 5 The Plain, St Clements – thus guaranteeing socialism at least some sustained public visibility in Oxford. The arrangement with English seems to have been a purely business affair, but Mrs Foy clearly had some left-wing political sympathies. She was a widow running a small shop in a poor part of the city and persisted in stocking *Commonweal* despite warnings from wealthier clients that she might lose their custom. 'I was talking to her today', Faulkner remarks, 'and reading the Commonweal has converted her: she did not need much conversion' (*WMC*, 9 November 1885). The third Oxford source of *Commonweal* was the bookseller, F.H. Plummer, of St Catherines House, Broad Street; for business reasons he had to keep his socialist sympathies under cover, but Faulkner none the less described him as 'the most active man' (4 May 1885). The group was by now managing to sell about forty-eight copies of *Commonweal* a month, with additional copies given away for general advertising and political purposes.

Meetings continued busily enough in 1886. In May the branch was discussing recent riots in Belgium. On 5 August Faulkner lectured to it on 'Free Trade, or the Man versus the State'. In early December they were discussing Joynes's *Socialist Catechism*, and at the end of the year *Commonweal* gives us a vivid glimpse of the Oxford branch in an item titled 'Town and Gown' by Ph. W. (Philip Webb presumably), who begins: 'Having an engagement a little time back whereby I was obliged to go to Oxford, I was able so to time my visit that I should be there on the evening of the usual weekly meeting of the Oxford branch of the Socialist League'. Webb dines in college with Faulkner, whose colleagues refer to him 'in a half-jocular half-cynical way as "Dynamiter"' (an improvement, one can't help thinking, on the earlier ridiculous nickname 'the Fogger'), and the two men later proceed to the League meeting in Pembroke Street. 'The Temperance Hall is a good enough and airy room, not so large as to look dismal with a small meeting, and yet with space to hold a hundred or more, easily.' On the evening in question some twenty-five people, including two or three women, turned up for a discussion on the topic 'For lack of knowledge', more particularly the lack of knowledge of 'how others live and feel'. After a paper given by a 'known comrade', 'one of the undergraduates spoke, and without regard to the possible consequences to himself. There was considerable freedom of speech from the more distinctly "working men," and illustrations were vigorous and greatly amusing, so that we were in no way dull' (*C*, 4 December 1886, 284–5).

The branch was at this point contributing to a left-wing undergraduate culture lively enough to win over even some unlikely converts, as we can see from Peter Jones's account of Percy Dearmer, who 'had arrived at Christ Church in October 1886, an ardent Conservative and Primrose Leaguer. Within months, influenced by the historian York Powell, he had read William Morris, Ruskin, and the rest. Dearmer became a devoted [F.D.] Maurician, decorated his college rooms with Burne-Jones and Morris tapestries, and dressed outrageously in loud checks and bright suits', though he involved himself in the Oxford Guild of St Matthew rather than Morris's Socialist League and subsequently went on to be a major figure in the Church Socialist League from 1906 (Jones, 249).

On 6 January 1887 a jovial note enters the Oxford Socialist League reports. The branch held a social gathering, at which sixty members and friends sat down to tea. The socialist speeches this time were, blessedly, 'short', and there was dancing and singing to enthuse the troops. In an 1885 issue of *Commonweal* Morris had cited John Ruskin's remark that 'A cause which cannot be sung of is not worth following' (*J*, 10), and his own socialist verse had set out to provide such materials; it is therefore no surprise to find that at the Oxford branch's festivities Morris's 'March of the Workers' and 'England Arise' figured prominently. Membership now stood at about thirty.

Serious business resumed with a visiting lecture from John Mahon on 'The Paths to Socialism' on 29 January. The audience was good, the opposition 'very weak', and fourteen shillings and threepence was collected in support of comrades in Norwich. Mahon himself, reflecting on his national tour in the following issue of *Commonweal*, gives us a helpful sketch of the health and prospects of socialism in Oxford as he sees them:

At Oxford, the audience was fairly large and very appreciative. The only opposition was from a gentleman troubled with some ancient ideas on Free Trade, who entered into a glorification of Cobden. The branch seems fairly active, and although not large its members are steady and reliable. Very few students attend the meetings, most of those with Socialist leanings prefer to work in the semi-Socialist societies, of which there are several in the Colleges. Oxford has no very large body of workmen, and a general spirit of flunkeyism pervades the poorer class; so that a very strong Socialist movement is well-nigh impossible there at present. Still the Branch is in a healthy condition, and will keep the cause alive. (*C*, 5 February 1887, 45)

Mahon gives shrewd pointers here to a Marxist analysis of the difficulties of establishing revolutionary socialism in Oxford. After the University saw off a proposal to site the Great Western Railway workshops near the city in 1865 (they went to Swindon instead), there was no large-scale industrial employment in Oxford until the expansion of the car industry after the First World War, and one could hardly conjure a militant proletariat into being from the small local factories that did exist. The University remained the largest employer in this period, which no doubt accounts for the 'spirit of flunkeyism' in Mahon's social analysis. Though both University and city did feel the impact of the 'Great Depression' of the 1880s, C.J. Day has argued that 'the University's resurgence shielded Oxford from the protracted decline which the agricultural depression inflicted on its rival [Banbury] in the north of the county' (*HUO*, VII, 1, 458). There was, moreover, a dense network of middle-class philanthropic organisations designed to help the neediest members of Oxford's population, with the wives of prominent Liberal academics such as Green, Toynbee, Müller and Nettleship playing notable roles; the Oxford Working Girls' Club, for example, designed to entertain and educate factory girls, was set up in 1887, right in the midst of the Oxford Socialist League's efforts to radicalise them.

In early May 1887, however, the Oxford branch was looking inward rather than outward as it discussed internal dissensions within the League, presumably in the run-up to the third annual conference at the end of the month, and Faulkner gloomily refers to 'our difficulties' over such issues as trade unions and parliamentary action (*WMC*, 18

May 1887). Yet the policy disputes do seem to have got settled, with Faulkner reporting to Joseph Lane on 18 May that the Oxford branch had 'refused to have anything to do with Parliamentary action … The opinion was almost unanimous against having anything less than Revolution. The very idea of reform is to keep present institutions going. For my own part I think all such movements as "8-hours a day" are just as reactionary as allotment schemes … It is the Tories who, if they had any brains, would promote such half-hearted legislation' (E.P. Thompson, 420). There could hardly be a more forthright statement of Socialist League purism.

The Oxford Branch goes underground in *Commonweal* for much of 1887, and when it next resurfaces, in a report of a meeting held on 23 November, ten days after Bloody Sunday in London, it is combining its forces with the Russell Club and Social Science Club, perhaps as a way of trying to win some undergraduates over to the socialist cause. The Reverend C.L. Marston spoke to the three organisations on 'The School, the Work, and the Workhouse, which are the lot of the Kentish Peasant, and the way to amend them', which suggests that the branch's interest in the conditions of agricultural labourers remained active. The League and the Oxford branch of the Guild of St Matthew were not the only forums for socialist debate in these years, however, for in December 1887 Edward Aveling returned to Oxford to address the Liberal Club on socialism.

The year 1888 opened with the usual Oxford branch New Year's party on 11 January, with music, song and dancing; so successful was the event that a profit of five shillings was made, which was donated to the *Commonweal* fund. February of this year saw a bold attempt to solve the perpetual problem of newspaper sales in Oxford, with the branch deciding to take to the streets to sell *Commonweal*. However, as Faulkner glumly reported in the wake of this experiment: 'we only managed to sell about 1½ doz the first week & only 2 or 3 last week – People say "Oh! What a little bit for a penny, & no news either". They must have their murders & adulteries etc etc, or they are not satisfied' (*WMC*, 21 February 1888).

Commonweal for 22 September 1888 contains one of Faulkner's last contributions. Headed 'Socialism at Oxford', it announces that 'our

comrades at Oxford are beginning to find that the town is as reactionary as the University, and are beginning to suffer for being Socialists.'
He notes that a Radical manufacturer had sacked some of his workmen
because they kept 'bad company' – the bad company in question of
course being members of the Socialist League. Faulkner himself, in the
heady days of early 1885, may have relished persecution when local
publicans refused to hire out rooms to the fledgling Oxford branch, but
clearly persecution from employers was a very much more serious business for working-class members or sympathisers of the League. During
a legal case against the same manufacturer by some of his employees,
the attorney for the defence 'asked the claimants whether they were
members of the Socialist League, and he did his little all to raise a
prejudice against Socialists by handing up to the bench copies of *Justice*
and *Commonweal*' (*C*, 22 September 1888, 302). We do not have any
record of the Oxford branch involving itself in local industrial actions,
but clearly the employers had taken note that it was active in the city
and were determined to stop it in its tracks.

In addition to hostility from local employers, the Oxford branch en-
dured a devastating blow when Faulkner suffered a stroke on 3 October
1888, three days after lecturing at Kelmscott House in London. Some
Morris biographers have seen Faulkner's occasional prostrations during
his Iceland trips with Morris in 1871 and 1873 as early indicators of the
illness that would eventually strike him down, yet he had been well
enough to travel to Norfolk and speak three times (once on education,
interestingly) during the strenuous socialist demonstrations in the city
on 12 and 13 August 1888. And certainly whatever his own intermittent
doubts about his leadership capacity, he had been the driving force of
the Oxford Socialist League from the beginning, and it was in danger
of being left entirely rudderless without him.

The Oxford branch submitted no detailed reports of activities to
Commonweal after January 1888, though the newspaper did still carry
brief announcements of weekly Wednesday meetings in the Temperance
Hall. From June 1889, however, a significant scaling down of activity
begins, for the branch's meetings are now announced as being held on
the first Friday of each month only. The Oxford Labour Club pamphlet
Red Oxford claims that in May 1889 the Oxford Socialist League branch

rejoined the Social Democratic Federation (Ashley and Saunders, 5). Perhaps it did, or perhaps it only partly did, thus leaving a rump of League members who had decided to carry on with monthly rather than weekly meetings; 'W.Ogden (Oxford branch)' appears in a list of proposed speakers for the Norwich event in August 1888 (*C*, 248), so perhaps he had sufficient local stature to sustain the League in Oxford post-Faulkner. In a letter to his daughter Jenny of 30 August 1889 Morris mentions that he has 'tumbled upon Ogden of the Oxford branch of S.L.' at Oxford railway station and travelled with him to London: 'we talked about the strikes wherewith he was much excited' (*CL*, III, 93), so it appears that Ogden was still at this point thoroughly engaged with local socialism and that the great Dock Strike of that year was having its reverberations amidst the dreaming spires as much as anywhere else.

However, in September 1889 *Commonweal* ran a list of the provincial stockists that were carrying the paper; Oxford does not feature in the list, so it appears that Faulkner's indefatigable efforts to get the paper established in local newsagents had not been effectively sustained beyond his stroke. Announcements of monthly meetings continue through 1890, 1891 and into 1892. Whether they corresponded to significant socialist activity on the ground in Oxford we cannot be sure, though there seems to have been enough of an Oxford branch left in existence in 1890 for the Hammersmith branch to bother writing to it and other surviving groups to announce its secession from the now anarchist-dominated Socialist League (E.P. Thompson, 571). The final Oxford announce-ment, in a *Commonweal* now declaring itself 'A Revolutionary Journal of Anarchist Communism', appears in the issue of 26 March 1892, after which the Oxford branch of the Socialist League, if it did still exist in any meaningful way, fades entirely from historical visibility. The only available organised option for socialist undergraduates for the next few years would be the Christian Socialism of the Guild of St Matthew or, from 1893, its successor body, the Oxford branch of the Christian Social Union, with its tepid policies of consumers' 'white lists' and 'Christian shopping'.

Charles Faulkner himself had died a month earlier, on 20 February 1892, though, as chance would have it, A.J. Carlyle, an undergraduate member of the Marx Club who had once read a paper on 'Population and

Socialism' to the Oxford Socialist League, was elected as a Fellow of University College in 1893 and played an important part in University left politics thereafter, so the flame of socialism at least continued to burn brightly in Faulkner's own college. Edward Burne-Jones was convinced that it was Faulkner's revolutionary politics which was responsible for his illness and death: 'Poor Charley Faulkner should never have been in for that vulgar row and turmoil – he was much too delicate minded and sensitive for it all ... Oh yes, it killed him, by the most painful of deaths, a terrible one lasting for years' (Lago, 92). But this is the assessment of one who had never had any sympathy with socialism, Morris's or anyone else's. J.W. Mackail in his Morris biography concurs with Burne-Jones, arguing that it was 'the work and all the load of toil and obloquy' entailed by Faulkner's socialist campaigning that eventually 'acted with dangerous and finally fatal result on him' (II, 218). But this is the voice of an Arnold Toynbee supporter who, as we shall see later, felt that Matthew Arnold's social thinking was on a more promising line than Morris's own.

I have tried to show above that Faulkner found the hurly-burly of socialist politics exhilarating as well as at times oppressive: he coped well with his press notoriety of early 1885, and was impressively devoted to the collective well-being of the Oxford Socialist League branch. Socialism for Faulkner, as we have noted, was a welcome escape from the miserable dreary twaddle of academic life, but it may in fact be that he found university life considerably more onerous than this dismissive remark suggests. In *Commonweal* for 10 March 1888 Morris reported that 'A very old friend, who has for many years been engaged in tuition at Oxford, has told me that the pressure there has enormously increased since I was an undergraduate' (*PW*, 603). The building of a new Master's lodging at University College in 1876, for example, for which Faulkner was responsible as bursar, turned out to be, in Peter Howell's term, a 'nightmare' for him as costs spiralled out of control (*HUO*, VII, 2, 750). So if we are compiling an unprejudiced checklist of the stresses that took their toll on Charles Faulkner's well-being, it is entirely possible that life as an Oxford don would have to feature high among them.

In a survey of the political events of 1887 Morris noted that 'in Russia the universities are closed in order to damp down the revolutionary fire spreading so swiftly among the students' (*PW*, 327). No doubt he did not, even in his most utopian moments, expect Socialist League successes of this magnitude at Oxford in the campaign there of the mid-1880s. Yet a lively socialist branch had been established in an unlikely environment and, even if it could never quite lay claim to the dignity of constituting a 'new Oxford movement', it did at least bravely bear the red flag for a few difficult years and planted political seeds which, as we shall see, would bear fruit in the life and writings of G.D.H. Cole in Oxford in the twentieth century.

FIVE

St Mary's Church, 1893

St Mary's spire still stood secure.

'Oxford', *Oxford and Cambridge Magazine* (April 1856, 255)

E ven during his most intense phase of socialist activity in Oxford in
1885 Morris had not entirely neglected his architectural campaigns
in the city. On 20 November, just ten days after his third lecture there
that year, he wrote angrily to the editor of the *Daily News*: 'I have
just read your too true article on the vulgarisation of Oxford', and he
launched into yet another stinging attack on Oxford's failure of guardi-
anship of its ancient buildings (*CL*, II, 493). After a year in which, as
Morris had announced to the eighth annual meeting of SPAB in June
1885, the Society had scored some successes, Oxford was clearly proving
as intractable a problem as ever. The agricultural depression of the 1880s
may have shifted Oxford University's social sympathies towards the
poor in the early years of the decade, but it had precious little effect on
the frenetic pace of new building in the city, which 'was at its greatest
in the 1880s and 1900s' (*HUO*, VII, 2, 762).

Yet the destruction of ancient buildings was only one, and perhaps not
the central, point being made by the anonymous author to whose letter
Morris was responding. I give his letter in full here, as a way of measur-
ing the distance between his concept of vulgarisation and Morris's:

Any Oxford poet might write a sad series of poems called 'Oxford Revisited.' Every six months he might go up and add a new elegy, or satire, as he preferred. The accumulated horrors of 'New Buildings' do not need to be described. One, at the corner of the Broad and Holywell, may cause the tear of sensibility to moisten the pavement. On the other hand, the laying out of a house with at least seven gables, inside the front lawn of Trinity, seems at present an advantage, unless the beautified old house is blocked out again by some modern performance, 'very late and excessively debased.' But the worst offence, and the most wanton of all, is the hideous ruin of the old view from Parson's Pleasure. As you enter the walk called Mesopotamia, by the Cherwell, you used to see, across the fields, a charming grey old village, and beyond that, and above a light blue curtain of smoke, rose the towers of New and the Dome of the Radcliffe. This was the best aspect of modern Oxford. It is irretrievably destroyed. The fields (foggy, one might think, and feverish) between the Cherwell and the town are being built over. The view is being first cut up, and then shut out, by the celebrated modern Oxford villa. Worse, if worse may be, remains. A low and bright red brick wall cuts across the foreground, and the foreground is now itself a hideous black ashen plain, divided into unseemly parallelograms by white lines. In fact, the foreground is a large and apparently swampy tennis court. The chances are that the floods of Cherwell and the white mists will prevent the villas from being 'eligible.' But who can praise the conduct which thus helps in the daily destruction of 'that sweet city with her dreaming spires'? At Oxford they excite themselves about Vandalism at Venice. The Vandal is a great deal nearer home – in the favoured city of Mr. RUSKIN. Mr. PALGRAVE, Canon DIXON, and Mr. COURTHOPE would not, if all were made Poetry Professors at once, be too many to restore taste to Oxford. (*Daily News*, 18 November 1885, 5)

The initial emphasis on new building and the danger it poses to older architecture runs along familiar SPAB lines, but the main thrust of the letter is clearly elsewhere, aimed at house building on what we would now term 'greenfield' sites. The threat to Oxford's ancient architecture in such cases is aesthetic rather than literal, a matter of losing a charmingly picturesque view across the fields. With the reference to the 'celebrated modern Oxford villa', we have entered the whole debate about the rapidly expanding suburbs of the city – a debate which was certainly in the background of Morris's 1881 campaign in defence of Magdalen Bridge and which he did not find a successful way of addressing there. Preservation of the core of the ancient city at all costs was SPAB and Morris's uncompromising position in 1881, however much traffic and population pressures might have increased. They could not compromise this 'extremist' stance without, as they saw it, giving succour to the modernisers.

Morris's reply to the *Daily News* letter, in an issue of the newspaper dominated by the 1885 general election, has shifted its ground slightly from the Magdalen Bridge campaign or from the defence of Carfax Church which was engaging SPAB between 1884 and 1885 (see the eighth annual report on this). Prompted by the author's reference to Holywell Street, and presumably by his own two visits to it as socialist lecturer in the course of the year, Morris this time defends a more homely Oxford against the modernisers: 'I wish to ask if it is too late to appeal to the mercy of the "Dons" to spare the few specimens of ancient town architecture which they have not yet had time to destroy, such, for example, as the little plaster houses in front of Trinity College or the beautiful houses left on the north side of Holywell Street. These are in their way as important as the more majestic buildings to which all the world makes pilgrimage' (*CL*, II, 493). There was in fact new building going on in Holywell Street even during Morris's 1885 lecturing campaign there, with Basil Champney's new range of undergraduate 'sets' and their accompanying tutor's house going up on the south side of the street in 1885–86, and subsequently a sizeable hole was punched in the row of houses on the northern side with the construction of Mansfield Road in the 1890s.

Morris's next epistolary intervention in Oxford debates took an unexpected direction. Instead of architecture he engaged his old university (at least initially) on the issue of literary studies, almost as if he wanted to air some of the views that his refusal of the Professorship of Poetry in 1877 had silenced. In 1885, while Morris was busy trying to create a socialist Oxford movement, the University had established the Merton chair of English Language and Literature. Though some of the leading men of letters of the day, including Edmund Gosse, George Saintsbury and A.C. Bradley had applied for the post, it had been awarded to

Arthur Sampson Napier, an Anglo-Saxon specialist. When it looked as though a planned School of Modern Languages might acquire a similar philological rather than literary bent, John Churton Collins, an Oxford University extension lecturer of strong Arnoldian leanings, and the *Pall Mall Gazette* together launched a campaign to persuade Oxford and Cambridge to take the teaching of literature seriously. Collins sent out a questionnaire to leading cultural figures, seeking their support for the study of literature at the ancient universities; more than forty replies, including Morris's, were printed in the *Pall Mall Gazette.*

From Churton Collins's viewpoint, Morris was certainly one of the awkward squad, with sympathies clearly tending towards the philological. 'As to the Merton Professorship', Morris wrote, 'I think the University did all it could in the matter, because philology can be taught, but "English Literature" cannot.' He will have no truck with a proposed professorship of English Literature because such a focus on criticism at the expense of the study of the historical evolution of English language and literature will in his view lead to subjectivism, intellectual vagueness, perverse ingenuity, and a truncating of historical perspectives; 'I fear that most professors would begin English literature with Shakespeare, not with Beowulf', remarks Morris, who would himself translate *Beowulf* just a few years later (*CL*, II, 589). He also took up the polemic in *Commonweal* where, after restating his point that English literature can be learnt but not taught and with the Brechtian *plumpes Denken* or 'crude thinking' that often characterises his contributions to the paper, he resoundingly declares that all the fuss is over 'the pushing of a great new *job* for all the clan of log-rollers in literature' (*J*, 231).

Having undermined Churton Collins's Oxonian campaign, Morris then uses the *Pall Mall Gazette* to advance his own more usual Oxford concerns; for 'if a new professorship is wanted, might not a humble one of mediaeval archaeology be established, with the definite object of teaching the dons the value of the buildings of which they ought to be the guardians' (*CL*, II, 589). Clearly the educational value of Oxford to Morris is sensory rather than intellectual, a matter of soaking up the implicit values of its ancient built environment rather than of academically studying texts and ideas there.

In 1890 the Reverend George Bainton, a Congregationalist minister in Coventry with whom Morris had already had a heavy-duty correspondence on socialism in early 1888, published *The Art of Authorship: Literary Reminiscences, Methods of Work, and Advice to Young Beginners, Personally Contributed by Leading Authors of the Day*. This attractive tome with its flowery blue cover may not, however, have been as innocent as it seems from its physical appearance, since there are some grounds for thinking that Bainton sought advice on writing from his 178 famous correspondents, who included Robert Browning, Thomas Hardy, Henry James and Mark Twain, without giving them any clue that their letters to him were intended for publication. At any rate, whether through such misunderstanding or not, Bainton elicited from William Morris in his lively reply a typically forthright statement on the education he had received at Oxford University: 'I was at Oxford before it was so much spoiled as it has been since by the sordid blackguards of "Dons" who pretend to educate young people there. I had the sense to practically refuse to learn anything I didn't like, and also, practically, nobody attempted to teach me anything' (*CL*, III, 154–5).

Such strong language was not likely to go unnoticed, or unreproached, in Oxford itself. 'J.E.K.' wrote in to the *Oxford Magazine* to remark that, as a recent translator of Homer's *Odyssey*, Morris must in fact have learnt his classics from somewhere, and to offer a challenge:

> will Mr. Morris submit to an 'antidosis' [change of places] of property, and exchange the paper shop (with socialism thrown in) for a year's trial of sordid profit as a don (blackguardism included), the gains to be handed over to the sacred cause of Anarchy? Till then we must ask ourselves why should a respectable tradesman and not undeserving poet allow himself to be tempted to write or talk indecent prose. (*OM*, 7 May 1890, 293)

This wry and measured Oxonian reproach was picked up, with a good deal more venom, in *The Speaker*. Dismissing Bainton as an 'egregious person', the anonymous author swiftly turns his fire upon the 'vulgar impertinence' of Morris's description of the dons:

> Shall we tell Mr. Bainton's young men that you, William Morris, have been the guest of these gentlemen you now fling filthy words at? Shall

we tell them that certain of these 'blackguards' have entertained you
and allowed you the use of a College Hall, and politely stifled their
yawns whilst you railed against their incomes? ... So, once again,
why 'blackguards'? Why not 'niddering wights,' or some other of the
opprobrious terms dear to the upholsterous Muse? (*The Speaker*, 17 May
1890, 536)

Morris took the opportunity afforded by the 'Why "Blackguards"?'
article to launch a ferocious attack in *The Speaker* of 19 May on what
he saw as the 'orgy of destruction' which Oxford University had been
engaging in against its own artistic and architectural heritage. 'Thirty
years ago Oxford was one of the most beautiful cities in Europe', he
asserts, but 'two-thirds of this beauty has now been destroyed'; and
it is not misguided restoration alone which has done the damage but
increasingly 'destruction for the sake of profit of which there has been
so much during the last few years'. So thorough-going has the process
been that the University authorities can now be fitly branded as 'the
greatest enemies that art has met with in this country during the nineteenth century' (*CL*, III, 157). It is when one comes to statements as
swingeing as this that one is inclined to look favourably upon Raymond Williams's critique in *Culture and Society* of 'generalised swearing'
in Morris's political prose (Williams, 151), yet in the case of Oxford
Morris could always give detailed instance after instance of the general
processes he is indicting.

For it is in Morris's view not only college buildings but town architecture too which has been devastated, and he returns, as in his 1885
letter on the vulgarisation of the city, to the defence of Holywell Street,
which 'contains the most of this old town architecture, and is still a
most delightful street, in spite of the gap caused by the gaunt and ugly
new buildings of New College', erected by Sir George Gilbert Scott
between 1872 and 1874. Trinity College may have saved the 'quaint and
characteristic houses' near its gates, which were also one of the objects
of Morris's concern in his 1885 letter, but this is a tiny victory in the
storm of demolition; and much more typical is the behaviour of Balliol,
'the destruction of whose buildings is such a disgrace to the ancient
House, such a gross insult to the "Famous Men and Fathers that begat
it"' (*CL*, III, 158).

Also of grave concern was the behaviour of Lincoln College, to the governing body of which SPAB had written to remonstrate against the sale by the college of the Mitre Tavern, which was about to be pulled down to make way for a new hotel (a hotel run by a London company for American visitors, according to an equally concerned report in the *Oxford Magazine*, 30 April 1890, 274). In criticising the college's decision, SPAB's 1890 annual report enunciates a key Morrisian tenet about Oxford when it argues that it was ancient buildings like the Mitre and their associations, rather than the learning acquired apart from them, which constituted the abiding influence Oxford had on those who spent part of their lives there. For such buildings, the report insists, make familiar and give actuality to former arts and customs in a way that nothing else can.

Standing back from the detail of the three letters of 1885, 1886 and 1890, we can see that a new term has entered Morris's anti-Oxford lexicon:

> Oxford 'culture', cynically contemptuous of the knowledge which it does not know, and steeped to the lips in the commercialism of the day. (20 November 1885, *CL*, II, 493)

> In the thirty years during which I have known Oxford more damage has been done to art (and therefore to literature) by Oxford 'culture' than centuries of professors could repair … to attempt to teach literature with one hand while it destroys history with the other is a bewildering proceeding on the part of 'culture'. (1 November 1886, *CL*, II, 589–90)

> I am most grieved to hear the current report that this remnant of Oxford before the age of 'Culture' is threatened with almost complete destruction. (19 May 1890, *CL*, III, 158)

Raymond Williams in *Culture and Society* gives us a necessary pointer here: 'Morris's principal opponent, in fact, was [Matthew] Arnold. The word "culture", because it is associated in his mind with Arnold's conclusions, is usually roughly handled' (Williams, 151). We must accordingly spend some time tracking Morris's developing responses to Arnold's work in the late 1870s and 1880s.

Both Matthew Arnold and William Morris were, as it happens, nick-named 'Crab' in infancy, and both developed a passion for angling that lasted throughout their lifetimes. Both were educated at Oxford, which, crucially, plays a continuing role in the subsequent literary imagination and cultural theory of both men. The history of adult relations between them seems to begin in 1869, with F.S. Ellis sending out to Morris in Bad Ems, Germany, a copy of the August issue of *Temple Bar* containing an article by Alfred Austin on the poetry of both men. In his reply to Ellis, Morris responds to some of Austin's criticisms of himself, but without broaching the topic of Arnold's poetry – though he was many years later to refer to Arnold's 'genuine, though not copious poetic gift' (*J*, 69).

Morris's political response to Matthew Arnold begins to take shape in the wake of the latter's lecture on 'Equality', published in the *Fort-nightly Review* in March 1878. Equality as Arnold defines it in this text is emphatically social equality rather than formal equality before the law, and though he dismisses socialist and communist politics as pro-pounding too low and material a standard of well-being, he none the less insists that the gross inequalities of contemporary British society are profoundly denaturing its attempts at civilisation. The problem, as Arnold sees it, lies in the law of bequest. Whereas France, under its Code Napoléon, restricts the freedom of bequest in order to break up large landed estates, Britain has no such restrictions and thus the inequality inherited from the Middle Ages can perpetuate itself across the generations. Though Arnold proposes what he regards as beneficial constraints on bequest in this country, he also concedes that 'evidently these are not questions of practical politics ... No, the matter is at present one for the thoughts of those who think' (Super, VIII, 305).

In an unpublished lecture which May Morris dates as 1880, Morris gives his public response to Arnold's text; for 'if I had not read his article on Equality in the *F[ortnightly] R[eview]* I doubt if I should have had the courage to say a good deal of what I have already said to you: I hope you will all read that admirable paper of his' (*AWS*, II, 69). In fact, behind such gestures of fulsome public praise Morris's view of Ar-nold's argument was more nuanced. In a letter of March 1878 he thanks

Thomas Wardle for sending him Arnold's lecture, 'with the main part
of which I heartily agree', and continues:

> the only thing is that if he has any idea of a remedy, he dursn't mention
> it: I think myself that no rose-water will cure us: disaster & misfortune
> of all kinds, I think will be the only things that will breed a remedy: in
> short nothing can be done till all rich men are made poor by common
> consent: I suppose he dimly sees this, but is afraid to say it, being,
> though naturally a courageous man, somewhat infected with the great
> vice of that cultivated class he was praising so much – cowardice to
> wit. (*CL*, I, 454–5)

It is this sharper assessment of Matthew Arnold which tends to
predominate in the pages of *Commonweal*, particularly after he accepted
a Civil List pension of £250 in August 1883 and thereby became in
Morris's view a decidedly establishment figure. In the May 1886 issue
Morris declared that Arnold's recent paper on the Irish Question in *The
Nineteenth Century* showed 'wither-ward "Sweetness and light" are drift-
ing … to wit, declaring formally for Reaction, as perhaps a pensioner is
bound to do in the long run'; it is sad indeed, he continues, 'that culture
should greatly ignore the struggles and aspirations of the greater part of
humanity, and elect at last to live and die in a flunkey's coat' (*J*, 69–70).
The assault continued in an article on 'Free Speech at Stratford' in June:
'To make the world outside Respectability one huge prison is the darling
wish of the Respectables, from Matthew Arnold the pensioner down to
some petty vestry tyrant at Stratford. Sweet alliance of the Superfine and
the Bumble!' (*PW*, 152). It was resumed, again on Irish issues, in 1888,
with Morris announcing that 'Mr. Matthew Arnold must go arm in arm
with Mr. Podsnap if he is to succeed now. The great preacher of refinement must back up the sordid wretches who steal two-thirds of the Irish
peasant's porridge with a long spoon indeed – viz., the whole power of
the British Empire' (*J*, 349–50). And it even began to extend to literary
as well as political matters, when J. Bruce Glasier attempted to rebut
Arnold's criticisms of the poetry of Robert Burns in his article 'Matthew
Arnold and "A Man's a Man for a'that"' (*C*, 29 December 1888, 411).

Various critics over the years have tried out comparisons of Matthew
Arnold and William Morris. Indeed, such comparisons feature right at
the start of Morris studies, in J.W. Mackail's biography of 1899. Mackail

sees both Arnold and Morris as making an epochal 'turn' to the working class around 1880. In his 1879 address to the Ipswich Working Men's College, '*Ecce, Convertimur ad Gentes*', Arnold argues for an 'approach to equality' in society, dismisses the middle class as incapable of regenerating itself, and urges his working-class audience to make the necessary changes themselves; thus far, Mackail concludes, Morris and Arnold are 'in complete agreement', though Morris's more boisterous temperament prompts him into activism, not just social commentary. But when Morris argues that his middle-class listeners should renounce their class and commit themselves to the socialist movement, his biographer bridles; 'to many it may seem', he demurs, 'that Arnold, and not Morris, in this instance pointed out the true path' (Mackail, II, 83–5).

Eugene LeMire gives us a suggestive footnote taking up the Arnold–Morris comparison in his *The Unpublished Lectures of William Morris*. He cites Morris in 'Of the Origins of Ornamental Art' to the effect that

> 'Absolute perfection in art is a vain hope; the day will never come when the hand of man can thoroughly express the best of the thoughts of man.' … This may be taken as Morris's answer to Matthew Arnold's injunction to become conversant with 'the best that has been thought and said.' It seems to be Morris's conviction that the best that has been thought has not and never will be said. 'Thought' means something more to Morris than cerebration, and his injunction is not to stop reading, but to start creating. (Lemire, 145)

The point, that Morris's is a richer and more holistic concept of the 'best' than Arnold's, is well taken, and we can reformulate it around the notion of culture.

For Morris's fundamental difference from Matthew Arnold is a matter precisely of the meaning to be given to that central Arnoldian term 'culture'. For Arnold, this is essentially an inward process of cultivation and self-perfection, its literary means being 'the best that has been known and thought' and its final outcome those qualities of 'sweetness and light', of the '*ondoyant et divers*', which characterise the man of Culture. For Morris, however, this ideal is inward-turning to the point of autism, and is damagingly intellectualistic. In his view, the essential means to culture are social and sensuous; they reside, as we have often had occasion to see in this discussion, in an osmotic responsiveness to one's built

environment, especially if, as in the case of Oxford above all, this is an
ancient built environment. At the beginning of his great 1883 lecture in
University College hall, Morris had appealed to his audience: 'first I must
ask you to extend the word art ... to the aspect of all the externals of
our life' (*CW*, XXIII, 164–5), and this powerful claim for extension is no
less applicable to the Arnoldian term 'culture'. For Oxford academics to
claim to represent the higher life of the intellect while they allow their
medieval environment to be destroyed around them is to privilege the
narrow Arnoldian sense of 'culture' (the study of texts) over its broader
Morrisian meaning (a holistic openness to the Ruskinian evidences of
the craftsman's creativity embodied in such buildings).

Several of Matthew Arnold's most celebrated purple passages evoke
Oxford, that sweet city with its dreaming spires which keeps whispering
to us the last enchantments of the Middle Ages, and one of the best
known of them evokes the voices of his undergraduate years there,
particularly that of John Henry Newman:

> Forty years ago he was in the very prime of life; he was close at hand
> to us in Oxford; he was preaching in St. Mary's pulpit every Sunday
> ... Who could resist the charm of that spiritual apparition, gliding in
> the dim afternoon light through the aisles of St. Mary's, rising into the
> pulpit, and then, in the most entrancing of voices, breaking the silence
> with words and thoughts which were a religious music, – subtle, sweet,
> mournful? (Super, X, 165)

It was one of the great disappointments of the young William Morris
and Edward Burne-Jones that their Oxford was bereft of the religious
passion which Newman's Oxford Movement had imparted to the University; but Morris, like Arnold, would also decades after his undergraduate
career find himself thinking of St Mary's Church, though not in the
mode of Arnoldian nostalgia but as an activist about to throw himself
into the debates raging around the building work taking place on the
church from the late 1880s.

To stand in front of St Mary's Church, with the Radcliffe Camera
behind one and Brasenose and All Souls' Colleges on either side, is to be
at the very heart of Oxford. For the medieval university, with no buildings of its own, adopted St Mary's as its academic and administrative
centre: scholars disputed here, the chancellor fined sellers of bad meat,

and, later, the trials of Cranmer, Latimer and Ridley for heresy partly took place in the church. Over the centuries the fabric of the building has been transformed many times, and the architect Thomas Jackson gives a detailed late-Victorian account of this process in his handsomely produced *The Church of St. Mary the Virgin, Oxford*; Jackson will, moreover, be a major player in Morris's campaign in defence of the church in 1893. The original Saxon church mentioned in the Domesday Book seems to have been rebuilt at the end of the twelfth century, with the famous tower and spire – the 'eye of Oxford' – added at the end of the thirteenth; the tower at this point stood away from the main body of the church at the end of a short north transept. The Congregation House, with its second storey serving as the university library, was added in the early fourteenth century, and a few decades later Adam de Brome's chapel was completed.

By the end of the fifteenth century, however, this early medieval structure had become unsafe, and by 1510 'the whole church, excepting the tower and spire, had either been rebuilt in the Perpendicular style of the day, or where the older structure was allowed to remain, as in the case of the Congregation House and the solar above, the exterior had been refaced in that style' (T. Jackson, 1897, 117). A new south porch, a 'strange mixture of Rococo Renaissance and late Gothic work' with its barley-sugar columns, was added in 1637 (128). The pinnacles and battlements of the new church had blown down in a great storm shortly after its construction, and the pinnacles of the steeple were only repaired in the early seventeenth century, in a Jacobean manner 'so unlike what a Gothic architect would have done' (133). Later during that century Dr Bathurst re-erected forty pinnacles on the main body of the church and paved the chancel with marble as part of a major classicising transformation of the interior.

Thereafter followed a long lull, until major work on the church resumed in the nineteenth century. In 1827 Thomas Plowman undertook a major refitting of the interior, subjecting Bathurst's classical scheme to a neo-Gothic reworking. In 1850–51, just before Morris himself arrived at Oxford, J.C. and C. Buckler rebuilt some 40 foot of the upper part of the spire, adding much higher pinnacles to it and replacing and repairing some of its medieval statues. In 1856, the year in which

Morris took his B.A. degree and started work in G.E. Street's Oxford office, George Gilbert Scott embarked on an ambitious repair of cracks in St Mary's steeple, tying the tower across with iron rods and screws in both directions. If the Society for the Protection of Ancient Buildings had been in existence at this point, it might well have approved of such necessary structural maintenance, but it would surely have been horrified at Scott's next St Mary's venture, in 1861–62, when the church was 'repaired and restored to such an extent that externally it almost became a new building' (148).

Buckler and Scott had both chosen Taynton stone for their rebuilding and restoration projects, hoping that it would prove more durable than the traditional Headington stone; but in fact this turned out to be a disastrous choice, and by the 1880s St Mary's Church was in a dire condition. As Jackson writes in his history of the church:

> finials and crockets began to fall from steeple and parapet, and a rapidly increasing pile of these fragments was heaped up in the little court between choir and Congregation House. Every storm brought something down, and the gutters were choked with the stone-dust washed by rain from the decaying face of the ashlar. On Sunday, March 17, 1889, the face of one of the statues fell and imbedded itself in the ground close to the north door, just after the Vice-Chancellor had passed in to attend University sermon. (150)

In the light of such evidences of decay and danger, the University in 1891 asked Jackson to examine and report upon the structure of St Mary's. Finding the church in a much more parlous condition than anyone had expected, Jackson had the building scaffolded and all stone in imminent danger of falling removed. An engineer, Wolfe Barry, was called in and concluded that the steeple was basically sound, even if its pinnacles were not, and Jackson's detailed plans for its reconstruction were published in the *University Gazette* and picked up by *The Times*, at which point, as we shall see, the Society for the Protection of Ancient Buildings began to concern itself in the matter.

Thomas Jackson was the dominant figure in Oxford architecture of the last quarter of the nineteenth century. Born in 1835, he had overlapped as an undergraduate with Morris; he studied at Wadham College, of which he became a Fellow in 1865. He was articled to George Gilbert

Scott and worked in his office from 1858 to 1861. Jackson's first visit to Italy in 1864 was an important moment in the process of turning his back on the doctrinaire medievalism of the Gothic Revival, and in 1873 he published *Modern Gothic Architecture*, criticising 'the school of purism and precedent' and advocating instead 'the necessity of a judicious eclecticism' (T. Jackson, 2003, 3).

Jackson's great breakthrough as an Oxford architect came in 1876 when he won the competition for the design of the new Examination Schools on the site of the Angel Hotel on the High Street. This building, used for the first time in 1883, drew a line under the Gothic Revivalism that had dominated Oxford architecture for a generation. Jackson memorably described the moment when he abandoned Gothic:

And so I set to work on my design in Gothic and the more I did the less I liked it. The thing wouldn't come at all, and I began to despair. Before my eyes seemed to come the haunting vision of Elizabethan and Jacobean work, and especially of those long mullioned and transomed windows at Kirby Hall in Northamptonshire; and finally I gave up all I had done and started again in a sort of Renaissance style and everything seemed to go smoothly. (T. Jackson, 2003, 111)

The Builder described the Examination Schools in 1887 as 'one of the best and most original of the recent English school for which it is so difficult to find a distinctive title' (9). *Faute de mieux*, Jackson's own name was called into service to evoke the vernacular style he had reinvented, and so it was that 'Anglo-Jackson' came into being as a mildly witty architectural label, a term subsequently immortalised in the opening lines of John Betjeman's poem, 'Myfanwy at Oxford': 'Pink may, double may, dead laburnum,/ Shedding an Anglo-Jackson shade'.

Thereafter Jackson became not a, but *the*, Oxford architect. As he himself cheerfully put it, 'I seemed to have become the fashion. It became a joke, when a man said his college was going to build, to say "Jackson of course!"' (T. Jackson, 2003, 7). 'The sheer quantity of Jackson's work in Oxford is staggering', as James Bettley sums up in his recent excellent account of the architect's work; it included high schools for both boys and girls, the front quadrangle of Trinity College, the High Street front of Brasenose, almost the whole of Hertford, including the Bridge of Sighs, the Radcliffe Science Library and the Electrical Laboratories, and the

'King's Mound' house in Mansfield Road. In Bettley's view, Jackson had by the late 1880s 'become something like the official University architect; he did some work or other, mainly restoration work, on practically every University building, from refacing the Bodleian to building the cricket Pavilion in the Parks' (5).

This being so, it is all the more disappointing that we do not have any record of Morris's response to Jackson's Oxonian work until the two men crossed swords over St Mary's Church in 1893. We have John Ruskin's vivid critique of the Examination Schools in 1884 – 'this black hole, with its nineteenth-century ventilation … in a style as inherently corrupt as it is unEnglish' (T. Jackson, 2003, 6) – but nothing from Morris, who could hardly have overlooked a new building as central and imposing as this (indeed, during the decorating of the Oxford Union in 1857 Morris had lived on this very spot, in one of the High Street houses subsequently pulled down to make room for the new Schools). It was, moreover, Jackson's choice for the Examination Schools of the yellower Clipsham stone from Rutland which began that 'de-greying' of Morris's Oxford that I noted in Chapter 2. Morris certainly knew something of Jackson and his work, since he lists him and correctly identifies his style in November 1881 as a possible member of his proposed council of architects who might report on Oxford's traffic problems during the Magdalen Bridge campaign: 'Penrose Street & Jackson: Classic, Gothic & Jacobean' (*CL*, II, 74). In fact, however, he might have found Jackson less obliging than he thought; for the latter had declined to sign the memorial that SPAB circulated on the issue.

All we do have by way of Morris on contemporary Oxford architecture are his negative remarks about George Gilbert Scott's New College buildings in Holywell Street that I cited above and his praise of 'Mr. Bodley's excellent new buildings at Magdalen College' in 'The Revival of Architecture', published in May 1888 (*CW*, XXII, 329). George Frederick Bodley, who had given Morris and Co. some of its earliest ecclesiastical commissions in the 1860s, and Thomas Garner had built the St Swithun's Buildings to the left of the medieval Grammar hall in Magdalen in 1880–84, and the President's Lodging to the right of it in 1886–88; these were widely viewed at the time as the best new college buildings in the city. We might also wonder what Morris made of the new Master's Lodging that Bodley and Garner had built at University College in the late 1870s under Charles Faulkner's bursarship, a building which Peter Howell describes as 'one of the most attractive examples of domestic architecture in Oxford' (*HUO*, VII, 2, 750). Morris once wrote jestingly to Faulkner of H.M. Hyndman that 'neither (as a Sec: of the SPAB) will I allow him to blow up any *old* building in Oxford' (*CL*, II, 236), with the implication that he might let him blow up some of the *new* ones; and it would be interesting to have a fuller sense of what the candidates for such Morrisian dynamiting might have been.

Morris's silence about Jackson's work in Oxford could not be expected to last when a building as precious as St Mary's Church was at stake. The Society for the Protection of Ancient Buildings appears to have had some earlier involvement with the building, as a reference to 'St Mary's Porch, Oxford' in the list at the end of its 1882 annual report indicates. Once Jackson's plans for the church's reconstruction had been picked up by *The Times* the Society's sensitive antennae began to twitch busily, particularly in relation to the medieval statues on the tower. Clearly, this was a much more straightforward issue for a SPAB campaign than Magdalen Bridge had been in 1881, since it did not involve those complex issues of urban expansion, transport technologies and mobility which the Society had never fully got to grips with in its first Oxonian battle. Nor were local commercial forces involved, as they had been with the tramway company in 1881. The St Mary's issue was rather, like the St Mark's campaign of 1879, one in which an appeal to the disinterestedly 'cultivated men' of Oxford University might hope to win the day. Here surely, if anywhere, Arnoldian 'culture' would rise to its own defence.

The Society's secretary, Thackeray Turner, wrote to Jackson expressing alarm at 'the report, which it earnestly hopes is ill-founded that the renewal of the statues has been decided upon', and enunciating a key SPAB principle: 'the authentic figures, however worn, will always be of extreme interest, while the most skilful imitations will be harsh when new, and misleading when time has softened them' (SPAB 2, 27 December 1892). Jackson replied caustically, lambasting the Society for basing its concern upon *The Times* without going back to his more detailed report in the *Gazette*. From the latter SPAB might have learnt, he

claims, that the 'more important parts [of the statues] have an antiquity
of only 40 years', having been repaired and restored in 1850–52 by J.C.
and C. Buckler during their work on the spire; and as for imitations,
'nor need I doubt our ability to do as well as our predecessors of 40
years ago, whose work you mistake for genuine sculpture of the 14th
century'. To add insult to injury, Jackson released the correspondence to
The Times, hoping in this way, presumably, to shame SPAB into silence.
(*T*, 28 December 1892, 10). In the view of the professional journal, *The
Builder* he had succeeded in doing just that. 'As usual, the Society has
got its facts wrong', it crowed, and after this, it concluded, 'the S.P.A.B.
will probably see the wisdom of letting Mr. Jackson alone for the future'
(31 December 1892, 516).

However, SPAB had no intention of letting Jackson off the hook. In
a letter to *The Times* of 3 January 1893, Turner concedes that two of
the statues date from the 1850s, but argues for two radical positions
if the genuinely medieval statues which remain absolutely cannot be
preserved *in situ*. Either their niches should be left empty, on the analogy
with classical textual scholarship, where 'good scholars have determined
that conjectural restoration is undesirable, and that it is better to leave
a gap in a Greek chorus than attempt to supply the missing lines',
or, alternatively, frankly modern new statues should be carved, which
made no attempt to fraudulently imitate their medieval forbears (*T*, 3
January 1893, 11). Jackson contemptuously dismissed both suggestions,
arguing that 'most people will agree that in their general effect the new
statues should preserve the decorative character and follow the lines of
those which formed part of the original design' (*T*, 5 January 1893, 7).
Sydney Cockerell noted in his diary for 6 January that Morris too had
written to *The Times* about the statues, presumably to give Turner some
heavy-duty back-up; but the letter, if actually written and sent, was not
printed (*CL*, IV, 47).

Behind the scenes SPAB continued to amass material which might
help with its campaigning. It made contact with C.A. Buckler to find
out exactly what he and his father had done to the spire and statues
in the early 1850s (discovering in the process that Buckler senior was
still living in Oxford and celebrating his one-hundredth birthday). It
wrote to W.H. Wheeler, a bookseller, stationer and photographer based

at 106 High Street, and secured photographs of the St Mary's statues taken from the top of his house. And it was trying to find out from other Oxford contacts when the meeting of Convocation would be held at which the University would decide the fate of the spire and statues; for, as Sydney Cockerell informed Turner, 'Mr Morris thinks of going down to vote' (SPAB 2, 29 January 1893).

In a further letter to *The Times* on 10 January, Jackson complained about the Society's purely theoretical campaign on behalf of the statues and contrasted this with 'the days and hours I have spent on the scaffolding at St. Mary's trying this stone and that in the hope of saving it, and in particular handling every bit of sculpture' (*T*, 10 January 1893, 11). He certainly had a point, as Cockerell in particular was aware, and SPAB's next move was therefore to commission a detailed report on the statues by two professional members of its inspecting committee. The inspection took place in late January, and the ensuing report was predictably bullish about the condition of the ten ancient statues, which represented St Mary the Virgin, St John the Evangelist, St Hugh of Lincoln, Edward the Confessor, St Cuthbert and five other archbishops and bishops. Though admitting they had been much repaired over the years, the report argued that there was 'no possible danger of any of the whole figures falling'. Of their historical importance to the church itself there was no doubt; for the statues and their niches 'are nearly all that justify the claim of St. Mary's spire to be still a work of the fourteenth century, so much has the main body of the work been "restored"' (Case, 17). Nor was there any doubt of their architectural importance to the country as a whole: 'Ancient free-standing statues in exterior niches, so frequent in France, are comparatively rare in England. It may fearlessly be said that this series of ten heroic-sized figures is second only to those on the west front of Wells Cathedral; they are priceless as the authentic record of the sculptor's craft in this country ... they may be left alone for future delight, or they may now be destroyed' (18). The Society sent copies of the full report to Jackson and the Vice-Chancellor, and got an abbreviated version of it published in the *Oxford Magazine* on 22 February.

It was in the wake of the SPAB report that Morris himself got fully involved in this campaign. It may have been his visit to France with his daughter Jenny in August 1891 which had sensitised him to the issue:

while out there he had been amazed at 'the amount of beautiful sculpture' lavished upon Reims Cathedral and noted pointedly that even where restoration work had been done on the building 'they do not here seem to touch the figure sculpture' (*CL*, III, 348, 343). Turner's letter to *The Times* of 9 January, which contrasts the restored statues of Westminster Abbey with those of St Etienne at Beauvais, 'through which, though every figure is shattered and headless, the undying beauty of the original conception still shines', certainly seems to have the weight of Morris's recent French experiences behind it (*T*, 9 January 1893, 14).

In late May, Morris wrote to Turner, in a letter which does not appear in Kelvin's *Collected Letters*, 'I am going to *see Jackson* next Thursday, and shall get some information out of him I hope. So will you kindly send me the report on the images' (SPAB 2, 20 May 1893). But this direct approach to the architect was not SPAB's only campaigning move at this point. It also printed a circular urging Oxford M.A.s to turn up to the next Convocation meeting to vote on the St Mary's issue, and with the eager assistance of Reverend E.S. Ffoulkes of Holywell Street and Morris's Kelmscott neighbour, Reverend Oswald Birchall, it distributed these as busily as it could. Henry Acland, who had spoken alongside Morris in the St Mark's Sheldonian meeting in 1879, replied sympathetically on 3 June but regretted that he could not make the meeting. Morris himself, on 2 June, endeavoured to get the Art Workers' Guild (of which Jackson was also a member) to pass a motion condemning the removal of the St Mary's statues, though in the end this campaigning ploy eventually petered out (Stansky, 165).

On 6 June 1893 Jackson, Morris and W.B. Richmond (who, as we have seen, had spoken alongside Morris in the Sheldonian in defence of St Mark's in 1879) travelled together from London to Oxford to examine the St Mary's statues and attend the meeting of Convocation at which their fate would be discussed by the University authorities. On the train journey, Jackson recalled, 'Morris was delightful and told us old stories he had been unearthing.' He then gives a vivid account of his and Morris's aerial inspection of the statues before the Convocation meeting:

> When we got to St. Mary's we scaled the tower and then had to get out on the scaffolding and walk around the outside so as to examine the statues. Richmond declined to come out and clung to the ladder,

saying it was like to give him gout as it was. Morris was bolder and came round with me. He was, I think, surprised to find how much modern work there was in the statues. Richmond said, 'I'll tell you what I should do, I should whip them all round with copper wire'; but old Axtell the mason said, 'But you know, sir, if the wire broke in one place all the rest would be useless.' Richmond then said he thought there was nothing to be done with them. Morris said they ought to be banded with iron to hold them together. I pointed to a piece, as big as my hand, which was cracked and nearly ready to come off, and asked him what he would do to prevent pieces such as that falling through his iron cage; for such a lump as that I showed him was enough to settle the business of a passer-by. 'I should put something below,' said he, 'to catch the pieces.' 'What would you put?' I ventured to enquire. 'Oh,' said he in a hurry, 'that I leave to you.' These suggestions did not seem to be very helpful. (T. Jackson, 2003, 206–7)

This was a poor performance by Richmond, certainly, who in 1881 had been boldly urging his students into the full-blooded direct action approach of tearing up the Magdalen Bridge tramlines. And did Morris, we may wonder, truly concede out on the scaffolding that there was much modern work in the statues? His own account of the aerial inspection, written to Philip Webb that same evening, is entirely uncompromising, declaring that 'I had a good look at the images, & fought Jackson at every point' (*CL*, IV, 47); so a self-serving slant may well have crept into the architect's retrospective narration.

What we can be sure of, though, is that after lunch at Wadham College Morris, Richmond and Jackson went on to Convocation. Jackson was eager to discover whether Morris would actually put his bizarre proposal of an 'iron cage with baskets below to catch the falling fragments' to the meeting and was then disappointed that he 'confined himself … to pleading for the "ragged regiment" (as he called it) generally' (T. Jackson, 2003, 207). Morris's contribution is given in some detail (and almost identically) in *The Times* for 7 June and *The Architect* for 9 June:

Mr. William Morris said it would be a pity to refer the matter to a delegacy; one thing was impossible, namely, to restore the fourteenth-century spire. He was in favour of repairing Mr. Buckler's work as the object of his boyish affections. But, further, he wished to plead for certain persons of whom hard things had been said, who were accused of having lost not only their hands but their heads. For these statues he was a thick-and-thin advocate. What difficulty there was in retaining them ought to be faced. The question was not whether it was desirable to retain them, but whether it was possible. But it was possible, and any necessary disfigurement would be better than destroying them or removing them to a museum, which would be equally destroying them architecturally. They were, in fact, the only fourteenth-century work remaining, and every step should be taken to preserve them. A rider should be added giving this direction to the architect. (*The Architect*, 9 June 1893, 373–4)

Morris's contribution at Convocation had in fact not been quite as unruffled as this account suggests. With the Reverend Oswald Birchall, the local correspondent for SPAB since 1887, sitting beside him, Morris had been interrupted as he began to speak by Professor Thomas Case, who objected that his exclusive focus on the statues was an irrelevance. The Vice-Chancellor, Henry Boyd, allowed Morris to continue, however, so that, as he wrote to Philip Webb, 'I got my word in, the point of which was that the preservation of the statues was far more important than the question of the arrangement of the pinnacles, which as a matter of fact is all that the dons are troubling their heads about'. Case, Morris concluded to Webb, 'seemed to me to be one of those knowing noodles of which Oxford always produces many' (*CL*, IV, 47). Noodle or not, Thomas Case, who was Waynflete Professor of Moral and Metaphysical Philosophy and a Fellow of Magdalen, had produced an impressive tome entitled *St Mary's Clusters: An Historical Enquiry concerning the Pinnacled Steeple* in the run-up to the Convocation meeting. Case was sympathetic to SPAB, certainly, and included its report on the St Mary's statues in his volume; but, as its title suggests, he was much more concerned about the fate of the spire as a whole.

We need not go into the complex debates around the spire and pinnacles at Convocation. With no record of the medieval original to work from, no putative reconstruction could be more authoritative than any other, and there was thus endless scope for argument between the four designs put forward. Morris voted for a return to J.C. Buckler's pinnacles of 1850–51, that being the steeple as he had known it in his own undergraduate days; but it was, clearly, the statues alone whose defence he had truly set his heart on. He kept up what pressure he could in the wake of Convocation through his Oxford correspondents. Writing to thank the historian Charles Boase for a book he had sent, Morris treated him to a long lecture on the importance of the St Mary's statues, arguing that 'they can be preserved if people are not too squeamish about the necessary means being quite obvious: I was going to say disfigurements, but I should not feel them so' (*CL*, IV, 54). When *The Times* on 10 June announced the composition of the Delegacy set up by Convocation a further opportunity presented itself, for it included the Reverend Henry Woods, President of Trinity College, who was a member of SPAB and had been an ally of Morris's in the 1881 Magdalen Bridge campaign. Woods therefore received the inevitable Morris letter on the subject, which asserts that 'he [Jackson] really wishes to keep them, & I gathered from my conversation with him that he rather shrinks from going to all lengths in banding & patching them'. Only a very firm steer from the Delegacy would, in Morris's view, adequately tie the architect's hands in this respect and thus ensure 'the preservation of the *only genuine remains* of St Marys Spire' (*CL*, IV, 56). Whether Jackson did indeed wish to keep the statues we cannot be sure. Such a desire hardly accords with the aggressive tone of his anti-SPAB correspondence in *The Times* in 1892–3, but perhaps Morris had to some extent won him round.

Yet in the end, as with Magdalen Bridge in 1881, the campaign over St Mary's statues was an Oxford battle that Morris lost. Though Jackson initially had hopes of saving the figures of St Cuthbert and St Hugh, he in the end decided that only one medieval statue, of an archbishop whom he speculated might be St Thomas of Canterbury, could remain in its original place, albeit with some patching up. Eleven new statues were carved by the sculptor George Frampton. Most of these, including Edward II, St Hugh and St Cuthbert, were modelled at the University's insistence as closely as possible upon the medieval originals, thus constituting exactly that modern forgery of the past which SPAB most deplored; Jackson himself had apparently hoped for a freer treatment. Three statues, which replaced Buckler's two statues of 1852 and one entirely unrecognisable medieval figure, were completely new; these gave Frampton the chance to show more of his own creativity and represented Walter de Merton, St John the Evangelist and St John the Baptist. All were cut from the yellower Clipsham stone, thus further eroding the 'grey city' of Morris's elegiac imagination. Moreover, Morris also lost the literary battle around the statues, since it is Jackson's magisterial 1897 history of the church which gives the fullest account of the treatment of them in 1893, and in this he portrays himself as the weightily authoritative and responsible architect, brushing aside 'the well-intended but hysterical outcries of societies and individuals who shriek whenever an old building is touched, without staying to inquire what reason there is for touching it' (T. Jackson, 1897, 160).

There is, however, a curious end to this story, of which Morris himself might to a degree have approved. For the statues that were removed from the spire of St Mary's were first stored in the Congregation House on the side of the church and later taken and installed in the cloisters of New College, which is where they can still be seen today. Morris may have deplored the 'gaunt and ugly' Holywell frontage of New College, but its cloisters had been from the start a sacred space to him: 'in their first term at Oxford Morris and Burne-Jones had spent many silent afternoons in [Merton College] chapel which they rated with the cloisters at New College as their chief local shrine' (MacCarthy, 72), and as we have seen the undergraduates at Morris's February 1885 lecture had taken him there late at night to enjoy their moonlit beauty. So sacred, in fact, were these cloisters to Morris and his immediate circle that his architect friend Philip Webb wanted his ashes to be scattered there after his death (the college authorities refused permission, however). So though Morris may have lost the 1893 campaign to preserve the medieval statues in their original niches, his ghost, if it should in Arnoldian fashion pass through Oxford enjoying the last moonlit enchantments of the Middle Ages, might not be too discontented at where his precious fourteenth-century artefacts have ended up.

SIX

The Oxford and District Socialist Union, 1895

During the summer of 1895 'the gradual failure of Morris's strength became clearly noticeable. Languor insensibly stole over him' (Mackail, II, 316). His career as a national lecturer was now at an end; he gave numerous talks in London in that year, but the great lecturing expeditions of the 1880s were long past. What energy remained was devoted more to the Kelmscott Press and the purchase of incunabula and illuminated manuscripts than to socialism. And as Morris's literary imagination gravitated back to the medieval period, so too in part, it seems, did his interest in Oxford. In August 1894 he was corresponding with Philip Lyttelton Gell, who had been a friend of Arnold Toynbee's at Balliol, played a key role in setting up Toynbee Hall and published a pamphlet on *Work for University Men in East London* in 1884. But Gell was now secretary of the University's Clarendon Press and Morris's letters to him are not about politics but rather about getting permission to use the text of W.W. Skeat's *Chaucer* for his own Kelmscott Press edition. A year later, in November 1895, we find Morris reading Hastings Rashdall's *The Universities of Europe in the Middle Ages*, a hefty work which in volume 2 part 2 paints a vivid picture of Oxford's intellectual vitality in the fourteenth century, and for which the ailing Morris 'expressed the highest respect and admiration' (Mackail, II, 321).

Yet one invitation did prompt Morris to venture out of the capital during this year of increasing ill health, and on 30 October 1895 we find him speaking again in Oxford, now for the last time, as he addressed the inaugural meeting of the Oxford and District Socialist Union at the Central Boys' School (now the bus station) in Gloucester Green. This was certainly the humblest of the various venues at which he had spoken during his long Oxford campaign, and indeed it had been designed by its architect, Leonard Stokes, precisely to blend in with its lowly surroundings. Morris's talk, 'What We have to Look For', had first been delivered to the Hammersmith Socialist Society on 31 March 1895 and is an important late meditation on the reformist and revolutionary paths along which contemporary socialism might travel. It was the wider working-class movement, rather than any University-based 'new Oxford movement', that Morris mustered his failing energies to address now.

While the Oxford branch of the Socialist League had long since gut-tered out into non-existence, new political forces had come into being at the University. Official Oxford culture had swung strongly behind the notion of Empire. Basil Champney's Indian Institute (now the home of the History Faculty) had gone up at the east end of Broad Street, an honorary degree was offered to Cecil Rhodes in 1892, and in February 1895 the *Oxford Magazine* adapted Sir William Harcourt's remark about socialism and declared that 'we are all "imperialists" nowadays' (6 Feb-ruary 1895, 196). The high period of Empire in Oxford may only have lasted, as Richard Symons argues, 'between Queen Victoria's Jubilee in 1887 and the 1914 war', but it was certainly a far cry indeed from the impassioned social concern and incipient radicalism of the early 1880s (*HUO*, VII, 2, 690).

On the other hand, in 1895 Sidney Ball, whom we have already en-countered in the wake of Morris's and Hyndman's 1884 visit to Oxford, had formed a local branch of the Fabian Society and he published a Fabian Tract on the *Moral Aspects of Socialism* a year later. However, he had been inviting Fabian speakers to Oxford well before the formal founding of the branch; Sidney Webb lectured there in the winter of 1886–7, Hubert Bland in 1892, and from autumn 1893 the Balls' house in St Giles became 'a hostel for early Fabian lecturers' (Ball, 74). It was due to Ball's influence, in Webb's view, that the Fabian Society 'was continuously represented in the University life and thought for some thirty years' (233). Was it to counter the impact of this emergent group, one wonders, that more militant socialists chose in the same year to launch the Oxford and District Socialist Union?

Morris had been invited to speak by William Hines, a college chimney-sweep who also kept a herbalist's shop, whom he had known since the early days of the socialist movement. May Morris recalled Hines warmly:

> Faulkner was not altogether alone in the wilderness, however: Oxford folk of that time and all who went there on Socialist business will recall one picturesque Oxford character, Mr Hines, the University chimney-sweep, who threw in his fortunes with us, and was not afraid to attempt the conversion of the Master of Balliol. Hines, by the by, took a great part in attempting to organize the agricultural labourers of Oxfordshire. (*AWS*, II, 177)

According to Sydney Cockerell's diary of 24 March 1892, Morris 'told good stories of Jowett', so it is conceivable that one of these colourful tales may have been of Hines's effort to convert Benjamin Jowett to socialism (cited *CW*, XIV, xvij). Not that Morris's anecdotes of the Master of Balliol were exclusively political, by any means; for in February 1887 he had been regaling his daughter Jenny with an account of an Oxford tea party at which Jowett was bested by his loquacious visitors (*CL*, II, 622). The hyperactive socialist here suddenly metamorphoses into a nostalgic Oxford graduate enjoying quaint tales of the eccentric academics left behind in the dreaming spires.

William Hines was an indefatigable political organiser; he was no great orator himself, but pulled a number of radically minded undergraduates and young dons into his efforts to mobilise the oppressed workers of the Oxfordshire villages. He had been active in agricultural trade unionism as far back as the 1870s, and was still recruiting for the National Agricultural Labourers' Union in 1890. After the successful London dock strike of 1889 the dockers' union decided to campaign in Oxfordshire and Lincolnshire, believing that if they could unionise and win improved conditions for agricultural workers, their members in London would not be undercut by desperate labourers driven off the land to seek any work they could find in the capital; and Hines, with his usual passion and energy, threw himself into this project too.

Oxfordshire was ripe for such a movement; for, as H.L. Samuel notes, it 'was in fact, with the exception of Dorset, the county with the lowest wage rates in England'. Samuel, who went up to Oxford in 1889, was one of the politically minded students who threw in his lot with Hines: 'Week after week two or three of us would join Hines, driving a dog-cart, and go out eight, ten or fifteen miles to the Oxfordshire villages, there to address in the open air a silent gathering of working-men – sometimes made the more timid by one or two of the farmers coming to the edge of the little crowd to note who was there. The movement spread fast' (Samuel, 16). Some improvements in rates of pay and working conditions were achieved, and the agricultural labourers also set up co-operative stores for their mutual benefit – Hines and Samuel often transporting stocks of tea, sugar and tobacco in their dogcart to provision them. The dockers sent their big guns into Oxfordshire for this campaign, including their charismatic leader Tom Mann, who spoke at a large public meeting in Oxford in December 1890. As the movement spread, so did its enemies become more active: not just farmers spying on meetings, but rowdy Conservative undergraduates screwing shut the doors of rooms in which Radical or socialist meetings were taking place in the city. On one such occasion, when George Bernard Shaw spoke at Magdalen College, fisticuffs ensued, with Hines in particular being 'rather roughly handled' (17).

Despite the optimistic beginning in 1891 – some twenty-two union branches were established in Oxfordshire that year – the movement fizzled out and disappeared by 1893, though it had certainly improved working-class self-confidence, and some of the union activists went on to get themselves elected to their local parish councils. Perhaps to console himself for this practical failure, Hines brought out in this year *A Penny Garland of the Songs of Labour*, gathering poems from Shelley to William Morris, with a preface by Frederick York Powell.

Hines seems at this point to have turned his attention from trade unionism to socialism and became a key figure in launching the Oxford and District Socialist Union. He certainly knew Sidney Ball, whose wife describes him as 'our dear old friend, Mr. Hines of Oxford', but while he may on occasion have addressed her husband in comradely fashion as 'Brother Ball' he was equally capable of taking an altogether tougher political attitude to the St John's don, referring to him caustically as 'that there Ball, he's nothing but a rusty nail' (Ball, 43), a comment that presumably marks the difference between Fabianism and socialism proper. Ball retaliated in a letter to his fiancée by describing Hines as 'the self-willed sweep who, indeed, gives to agitation what was meant for his wife and (very many) children' (68).

Hines achieves a minor form of literary immortality in Max Beerbohm's essay 'William and Mary' in *And Even Now* (1920), which narrates the adventures of a Morris-inspired socialist undergraduate at Oxford. The latter has bought deeply into his hero's literary as well as political enthusiasms; for the narrator remarks, 'Nor could I without yawning listen to more than a few lines of Mr. William Morris' interminable smooth Icelandic sagas, which my friend, pious young socialist that he was, thought "glorious." He had begun to write an Icelandic saga himself, and had already achieved some hundreds of verses.' Mildly risible the student hero may be, yet it takes a certain courage to be a socialist in the city depicted in the essay; for 'in 1890 there was only one other socialist in Oxford, and he not at all an undergraduate, but a retired chimney-sweep, named Hines, who made speeches, to which nobody, except perhaps William, listened, near the Martyrs' Memorial' (Beerbohm, 260).

Beerbohm's story is not the only fictional depiction of Oxford socialism, it would seem. The *Oxford and Cambridge Undergraduate's Journal* had informed its readers in March 1884 that '*The Gentleman's* [*Magazine*] has always a *pièce de résistance* to rely on in "Philistia". A story, of Oxford Socialism, in which the Socialists are nearly as silly as their prototypes at Oxford to-day' (6 March 1884, 288). I have not been able to track down this reference, however.

Morris's talk in the Central Boys' School was chaired by Professor Frederick York Powell, in whose rooms in the Meadow Building of Christ Church College, cluttered with Japanese carvings, old psalters and Parisian advertisements, Morris stayed that night. The next morning the two men examined medieval books in the college library together. Morris had known Powell for some years and gives a brief account of him in a letter to his daughter Jenny in September 1886:

> Yesterday Mr. Guerrault called wanting work; Mr. York Powell (who is working with Guðbrandr Vigfússon at Oxford) was with him … Powell is a very nice fellow, a good deal of a Socialist and very genial: he was

born & bred in Walthamstow, though a Welsh one of blood: he used as
a boy to come to Leyton House, he told me. (*CL*, II, 573)

Being a 'good deal' of a socialist is better than not being one, certainly;
but it is perhaps not the same as simply *being* a socialist. The question of Powell's politics is therefore one we shall need to return to. He
was indeed born in Walthamstow, as was Morris himself, but sixteen
years later than Morris, in 1850, and his family lived there for the first
fourteen years of his life. Leyton House was the residence of Morris's
mother, and it appears that she and Powell's mother were acquainted;
Powell visited her as a schoolboy and remembered her as 'very cheery
and simple-hearted, and extraordinarily sympathetic in [the] joy or
sorrow of young people (Elton, 234).

Powell's father was a commissariat merchant, and the son underwent
a conventional middle-class upbringing. He attended Rugby from 1864
to 1866, then completed his schooling at Bonchurch on the Isle of Wight
from 1868 onwards. But already distinctive interests were emerging. The
headmaster at Bonchurch wrote later that

> at an age when boys are given to decorating their schoolbooks with
> more or less libellous portraits of their masters, he had covered his
> with alphabets, or Runic scrolls, and he was beginning to work at Old
> French and German, and at Icelandic. One of his favourite books at
> this time was Dasent's *Burnt Njal* ... He had ripened early and thought
> for himself. When he came to me he already held strong agnostic and
> socialistic opinions. (11)

At the age of seventeen or eighteen Powell had already translated the
Icelandic saga of the Faroe Islanders, which many years later he revised
and published; and, as his awestruck biographer Oliver Elton notes,
he 'was no doubt almost the only English boy of his generation thus
engaged' (31). At this point William Morris had not even met Eiríkr
Magnússon, who was to be his own mentor in Icelandic, though when
he did, in 1869, he quickly made up for lost time.

Powell went up to Oxford in 1868 to study law and history and
joined Christ Church College at the end of his first year. His literary enthusiasms as an undergraduate included Swinburne, Whitman,
Rossetti, Shelley and Morris himself, though in later years he remarked

of Morris's poetry that 'he can't rise above the naïve melodic' (229). Oxford political life in the early 1870s was enlivened by European exiles. As a contemporary of Powell's notes, 'the Frenchmen came for refuge. Out of the wrack of Paris these Communards appeared, mostly unkempt and woebegone: but very gentle ruffians indeed' (19). Whether any of these figures had as transformative an effect on the young Powell as the Communard refugee in Morris's *Pilgrims of Hope* has on that poem's narrator, we do not know; but certainly Powell seems to have been well known in émigré circles. Another contemporary recalled Powell 'taking him to a small café on or near the site of the present Empire Theatre. It was full of foreign exiles who knew Powell and greeted him' (22).

In 1874 Powell became a lecturer in law at Christ Church, and the 'chief event of his mental life' took place when he met the little-known Icelander Gudbrand Vigfússon, who had been living in Oxford from 1866. Twenty years older than Powell, Vigfússon had come to England to complete the Icelandic dictionary begun by Richard Cleasby; it was published in 1874. His authoritative presence clearly gave shape and purpose to Powell's own boyish Icelandic enthusiasms; and 'together they formed and executed, as far as could be, the double purpose of promoting Icelandic scholarship and placing their results before all who could read English' (38). A formidable programme of scholarship and publishing resulted from this resolve. A weighty 200-page Prolegomena to the *Sturlunga Saga* was published in 1878, giving a compact survey of Icelandic literary history. An *Icelandic Prose Reader* followed in 1879. Powell's own article on 'Icelandic Language and Literature' appeared in the *Encyclopaedia Britannica* in 1881. In 1883 there followed *Corpus Poeticum Boreale*, the best-known of their labours, which gathered all ancient Northern poetry, together with translations and full commentary. The last piece of this impressive scholarly jigsaw was the *Origines Islandicae*, which includes the Book of Settlement and did not appear until 1905, a year after Powell's death; for after Vigfússon died in 1889 the heart went out of Powell's scholarly endeavours.

So when Morris wrote to Jenny about Powell in 1886, the latter had clearly established himself as one of the major figures in British Icelandic studies. Moreover, this appears by no means to have been his only visit to Morris in Hammersmith. Though Powell taught in Oxford, he lived in London and had moved to Bedford Park, west of Hammersmith, in 1881. Here he certainly moved in advanced cultural and political circles. He was well acquainted with the painter Jack Yeats (W.B. Yeats's father) and sat to him for a portrait; he was friendly with Sergius Stepniak, the exiled Russian revolutionary whose *Underground Russia* had a profound impact on William Morris in 1883; he often spent the evening with John O'Leary, the rebel Irish patriot. Powell was an Ibsen enthusiast and went to as many London performances of his works as he could; 'Ibsen is the boom here' he wrote cheerily in 1891 (131).

And Morris, for Powell, was certainly part of this avant-garde movement. In a talk given in Oxford after Morris's death he maintained that 'he had often gone to the house at Hammersmith, crowded with books, yet so "light and free from dust", where they talked about all kinds of things, especially literature'. He had also visited the Merton Abbey works with its founder: 'Morris had gone over there every day for the six months previous to our visit, but he was as pleased as if he had never been there before. He knew the work from the beginning of the process to the end, and that was the reason why it was so extraordinarily well carried out' (234). Did Powell ever inspect Morris's Kelmscott Press? We cannot say for sure, but in his later work for the Clarendon Press at Oxford he certainly took a lively interest in the physical side of book production as well as playing a more conventional academic and editorial role. An obituary in the *Oxford Magazine* noted that 'he admired the bookwork of Morris ... But he knew the points at which Morris had failed' (cited 217–18), and it would be intriguing to have Powell's own statement as to what those supposed points of failure were.

How did the two men view each other as Icelandic scholars and translators? We have no full statement of opinion on either side, though Powell's biographer, Oliver Elton, briefly tries out a comparison: 'that highly archaic and biblical element, which William Morris often mixed, with as lovely and unretarding effect as Spenser, into his own prose, Powell uses much more lightly and sparingly' (106). But we have stronger testimony of Powell's views of other aspects of Morris's work, intellectual and otherwise. Powell became Regius Professor of History at Oxford in 1894 and it was Morris's historical imagination that seemed then to matter most to him. A former student recalled 'how vigorously he praised the historical work of William Morris ... Morris, he said, was perfectly at home in the fourteenth century, and he would have needed no introduction to the Canterbury pilgrims' (208). In the 1897 talk on Morris, Powell remarks: 'As to *The Dream of John Ball*, it is a great thing to have an historic imagination so strong as to be able to present such a living picture of the past' (235). He had also supported, albeit passively, Morris's position over the restoration of St Mary's Church.

So when Powell took the chair for Morris's 1895 talk to the Oxford and District Socialist Union the latter must have felt that he had found the perfect partner for the occasion, someone who could perhaps fill the role that Charles Faulkner had once played in mediating between the academy and a wider socialist politics. And certainly Powell's radicalism comes through vividly in these years. We have already seen the dramatic impact he had upon the young Percy Dearmer in 1886, converting him from Primrose Leaguer to ardent Christian Socialist, and another former student recalled 'his blazing indignation against oppression, political or intellectual or religious, and his manly defence of the despised brought occasional bursts of eloquence into his lectures' (199). The novelist George Meredith noted after Powell's death that 'in France or Germany it was no novelty for a man of great learning and a distinguished professor to be in open sympathy with conspirators against the lords of misrule'; but in Oxford it was, and Powell had been such a man (225). While Morris attended socialist celebrations of the Paris Commune in London, Powell was giving a course of lectures on the Commune in Oxford. Indeed, Powell seemed to be gathering both the literary and political avant-gardes in Oxford. He had, for instance, chaired the notoriously disorderly meeting in March 1884 when Henry George tried to expound his land nationalisation views to a hostile audience in the Clarendon Hotel, and in the early 1890s he was instrumental in getting Paul Verlaine and Stephan Mallarmé to lecture in the city.

Moreover, Powell seemed to be forging links between the academy and a wider Oxford politics in his own personal life. Elton describes his position in Oxford as 'peculiar' and notes that William Hines was 'amongst his chief friends in the place' (421–2). An index of that closeness, as we have seen, is the fact that Powell wrote a short preface to Hines's collection of poems for workers in 1893.

Morris's speech was a successful inaugural event for the Oxford and District Socialist Union, as I shall argue below, but it was less successful in fortifying his chairman's political opinions. For worrying cracks had already begun to appear in Powell's socialist credentials. One student noted his remark that 'if socialism is to come it will do so gradually; the world is not yet [1894] ready for it, the reason being that people are not yet sufficiently trained in this direction' (166). A necessary debate about socialist tactics – gradualism versus revolution – seems here on the point of tipping over into a wholesale Tory fear of the masses. In the address on Morris in 1897 Powell was, Elton remarks, 'in accord with many of Morris's aims, but cared little for the method of propaganda, "speaking at street corners," which after all was not Morris's strength because he often spoke ineffectively' (236). But if one does not propound any methods for achieving socialism, in what sense can one really be said to be a socialist after all? And indeed the change in Powell was already by this point in full swing. By 1897, Elton informs us, 'he was already sealed a votary of the newer imperialism' (244); the Boer War 'made something of a crisis … in his political opinions' (258); and by 1899 the metamorphosis was complete, for Powell was now 'at many points an aggressive Tory, bursting often into angry fire, writing and speaking with vivid intensity, and refusing to argue' (262). His pamphlet *Thoughts on Democracy* is a fierce warning against the dangers of popular rule, and his admirable efforts on behalf of Ruskin College in Oxford seem paradoxically to have been motivated by the same spirit, with the new college being potentially 'the kind of antidote he desired to see to the risks of democracy' (307). In the last months of his life he became president of the Oxford University Tariff Reform League, an initiative aimed at imperial economic consolidation. If social being determines consciousness, in good Marxist fashion, then it would seem that the pervasive imperial culture of Oxford in the later 1890s ('we are all "imperialists" nowadays') had taken its toll on Powell's more progressive sympathies.

There was still some sympathy in Powell for Morrisian cultural ideals in these later years. When Sydney Cockerell wrote to him in 1899 asking him to support a movement for the protection of buildings in Oxford he responded positively, and his old Icelandic enthusiasms still flickered intermittently, finding a last expression in 1900 in a preface to Beatrice Barmby's *Gisli Surrson*. But the political sympathies with Morris had long since evaporated. We can accordingly see how well Morris's 1886 phrase – 'a good deal of a Socialist' – is weighted. Did he already have some inkling that Powell's commitment was not as deep-seated as he might have hoped or as Powell himself might have believed at that point?

The scene in the Central Boys' School on 30 October 1895 is neatly evoked in the *Oxford Chronicle*. The room itself was, in its opinion, 'largely inadequate for the purpose', though encouragingly for Morris and the organisers 'representatives of probably every class in the City were present'. The younger comrades seem to have decided to make quite an occasion of Morris's talk, sartorially speaking, with the *Chronicle* noting that 'sundry young lady "comrades" appeared in masculine-like skirts with red ties, others sported red bonnets, while in one case the distinctive badge was a flaming red blouse.' The young men, not to be outdone, turned up 'in what is understood to be the correct Socialist costume', though alas the paper does not specify what this is. Morris himself, in the *Chronicle*'s view, 'is no orator with a fine flourish of phrase, but is an able speaker in so far as an excellent delivery, coupled with a vocabulary of forcible, simple and pure English can make him so'. Though the newspaper only goes so far with Morris politically – its Radicalism stopping well short of his socialism – it none the less announces that 'it must be a privilege to have him as a leader'; and in a city which had so often accused Morris of not living up to his left-wing principles in his conduct of the Firm the *Chronicle* rather surprisingly concludes that 'in his business he has had the courage of his convictions' (*OC*, 2 November 1895, 5).

Morris's aims in his lecture were, he declared, quite modest: 'it is not prophecy that I am about to-night but a reasonable forecast of the few next moves deduced from the experience of the last few' (*AWS*, II, 358). Declaring that in the last five years the socialist movement has undergone a 'great change', he first looks back to the heady early days of the movement, of which his Oxford campaign of 1883–85 had, as we have seen, been a notable part. In those years socialists had been convinced that only violent insurrection could achieve their political aims, and police harassment of street meetings and the state repression of Bloody Sunday in 1887 reinforced this belief. But the young movement – that 'collection of oddities', in a colourful phrase Morris cites from an unnamed friend (359) – had not been able to make contact with the wider working class, even though it had its individual proletarian adherents.

Over the last five years, however, Morris continues ruefully, the whole idea of insurrection has been abandoned by the movement and exists only as the bloodthirsty dream of contemporary anarchism; gaining a socialist majority in Parliament is now assumed to be the responsible route to power. At the same time the movement has made headway among the wider working population. This development has also been noted by the Tory and Liberal parties, which have accepted that they may have to make some concessions to socialist demands. Morris remains deeply sceptical of 'all those measures for improving the material condition of the working classes without altering their position'. They amount in his view to feeding the dog with its own tail, bettering 'the condition of one group of workers at the expense of others: and thereby you make partial content out of general discontent' (Morris, 30 March 1895, 60).

But in the contemporary struggle between 'Commercialism, or the system of reckless waste, and Communism, or the system of neighbourly common sense' (61), the working-class movement seems unsure what its aims are; it stands poised between reformist and revolutionary demands, unable to focus the issues involved in the choice between the two directions. Hence it is that Morris 'should like to ask [the workers], before I say anything about your tactics and your demands, what it is you really want':

> I should above all things like to have a genuine answer to this question; setting aside all convention, all rhetoric and flummery, what is it that you want from the present labour movement? Higher wages; more regular employment? Shorter working hours, better education for your children, old age pensions, libraries, parks and the rest. Are these things and things like them what you want? ...
>
> If you *can* answer it, and say Yes, that *is* all we want: then I say here is the real advice to give you: Don't you meddle with Socialism; make peace with your employers, before it is too late, and you will find that

from them and their Committee, the House of Commons, you will get
such measure of those things as will most probably content you, and at
any rate all that they *can* give you without ruining themselves as they
phrase it. (62–3)

Such a reformist prospect hardly inspires Morris himself. 'I must own
that sometimes when I am dispirited I think that this is all that the
labour movement means: it doesn't mean Socialism at all.' But there
are other straws in the wind which bespeak a quite different kind of
political commitment at work among the population. The success of
Robert Blatchford's *Merrie England*, published in 1893 and (as Morris
modestly does not point out here) much influenced by Morrisian ideas,
is one such indicator. For 'the thousands who have read that book must
if they have done so carefully have found out that some thing better is
possible to be thought of than the life of a prosperous mill-hand … Self
respect, happy and fit work, leisure, beautiful surroundings, in a word,
the earth our own and the fullness thereof, and nobody really dares to
assert that this good life can be attained to, till we are essentially and
practically Socialized' (64–5).

Even if the labour movement does pursue the parliamentary direction
there will still be a great task of political education to be performed,
Morris asserts, for it will remain crucial to 'point out to the working-
men who feel Socialist sympathies that there are many measures which
may be for the temporary good of their class, which are but temporary
and experimental, and adapted only for the present state of things, and
that these are not for genuine Socialists to press forward' (67). The
task thus remains, as it had ever been for Morris, to 'make Socialists',
but crucially to shape them towards revolution rather than palliative
reformism.

After Morris had concluded there was 'a brisk fire of questions an-
swered with much point and brilliancy', according to *Justice* (9 November 1895, 60), but we have no record of what those questions were.

After his lecture to the Oxford Socialist Union, Morris spent the
night in York Powell's rooms in Christ Church, and the following morning the two men went into the college library to examine two medieval
books which Norman Kelvin has identified as Walter de Milemete's *Liber
de Officiis Regium*, a book of instruction for princes written for Edward

II in 1326, and the Desmoulins French New Testament of around 1280
(*CL*, IV, 333). As Morris turned eagerly from woodcut to woodcut in the
de Milemete volume he might seem to have regressed from activist to
undergraduate; far from seeking energetically to refashion his old university, he seems once again to be passively gawping in wonderment at
its medieval treasures. But that this is not entirely the case is shown by
a remark in a letter to Sydney Cockerell about the French New Testament, where undergraduate awe passes swiftly over into something more
active: 'the illuminations of most singular beauty & refinement. I wish
Rosenthal would find me one like it; I would buy it as an expiring effort'
(IV, 332). We are at once recalled to the fact that Morris in his last years
was an avid collector of medieval manuscripts and early printed books:
the admiring student has metamorphosed into the successful business-
man who has amassed a sufficient fortune to buy, if not Oxford's own
cultural treasures, at least rough equivalents to them. Indeed, in his
book-collecting Morris showed some interest in the origins of printing in
Oxford itself, acquiring in May 1893 a copy of John Lathbury's *Expositio
ac Moralisatio tercii Capituli Trenorum Iheremiae Prophetae*, which had been
printed at Oxford in 1482 by Theodoric Rood and Thomas Hunte (IV,
45). Rood had printed his first book in Oxford in December 1478, just
a year after Caxton had got English printing under way.

The motives for Morris's passionate collecting are various: a sensuous pleasure in the artefacts themselves which at times verges on the
obsessive, a sense of the books and manuscripts as an investment which
would financially provide for his wife and daughters after his demise,
a need for them as models and working tools in his own role as printer
and publisher at the Kelmscott Press. And it is here that we again begin
to glimpse a third relationship between Morris and the University of
Oxford, one which was adumbrated in his cataloguing of medieval missals for Edward Nicholson in January 1884. This third relationship was
never fully developed in Morris's lifetime, but it escapes the binary
opposition between Oxford-influenced undergraduate (the story commentators have usually told about Morris and his university) and the
Oxford-influencing activist (the story I have been concentrating upon).
The crucial episode here is neither political nor architectural but biblio-
philic; for on 28 November 1894 Morris and Emery Walker travelled

up to the Bodleian Library to see the thirteenth-century manuscript known as the *Douce Apocalypse*. It had been one of Morris's and Burne-Jones's most cherished medieval manuscripts during their student years – indeed, it is described by Mackail as Morris's 'ideal book' (Mackail, I, 40); and no doubt that youthful wonderment was reactivated on this visit too. But Morris's purpose was not simply to gape, nor even, as with the French New Testament, to dream up equivalents he might acquisitively purchase for himself, but rather to produce a facsimile of the *Douce Apocalypse* as a Kelmscott Press volume.

Sadly, this plan never materialised; it too remained, to borrow Joseph R. Dunlap's fine phrase, a Book that Never Was. Negotiations with Edward Nicholson about photographing the manuscript had opened in September 1894; there were complex to-ings and fro-ings about whose photographer should do the work; and finally in March 1895 Walker was given permission to send his own operative to get on with the job. But though the plan for a Kelmscott facsimile of the *Douce Apocalypse* did not get further than this, it does show a new relationship that was potentially opening between Morris and his alma mater, with the former now neither student nor activist, but rather co-producer, both receiving and simultaneously transforming the cultural treasures Oxford offers to him. The relationship, for whatever reason in the case of the *Douce Apocalypse*, foundered almost before it could get under way. But at least its possibility was sketched out, and had Morris lived longer there might have been other ways in which it could have been developed.

This is the moment to ask, finally, whether there are significant relations between Oxford and the Kelmscott Press, other than the obvious one of it being Morris's youthful love of the Bodleian's incunabula and manuscripts that is ultimately behind his move into fine printing in his last years. It has occasionally been claimed that the Daniel Press of the Reverend C.H.O. Daniel, Fellow of Worcester College, Oxford, from 1863, was a significant precursor of the Kelmscott Press. Daniel had been printing ephemera on a toy press from childhood onwards, and in 1850 he acquired a miniature Albion Press, which in 1874 he set up in his rooms at Worcester. Two years later he discovered the seventeenth-century Fell types, with which he printed one of his most admired works, *The Garland of Rachel*, in 1881. A year later Daniel acquired a full-sized Albion Press, on which more than fifty books and minor pieces were subsequently printed. Large claims have been made for his work, with Falconer Madan arguing that 'the use of the Fell type in 1877 and the production of the *Garland of Rachel* in 1881 may fairly be regarded as the first genuine signs of the Revival of Printing in this country' (Madan, 47).

'Was Morris familiar with any of the Daniel books?' asks William Peterson in his fine study, *The Kelmscott Press*. Peterson, as the most authoritative Morrisian commentator on this matter, notes that Morris 'never mentioned Daniel or his press' and concludes robustly that 'to see the Kelmscott Press as the direct descendant of the Daniel Press (as Madan suggests) is misleading' (Peterson, 36). In fact, however, matters are more complex than this and there is a web of connections between the two men. Daniel himself had first seen Morris in action in the Sheldonian Theatre in November 1879. Having decorated Worcester College chapel from William Burges's designs to produce one of Oxford's most important Pre-Raphaelite monuments, Daniel certainly had aesthetic interests strong enough to prompt him to attend a meeting in defence of St Mark's; but he also did a stint as Oxford correspondent for *The Times*, so it may possibly be his report of the Sheldonian gathering – and of subsequent Morris Oxford appearances – that we read in that newspaper. He, like Morris, had a profound love of the Upper Thames countryside: he and his family often travelled those waters in their houseboat and during the university summer vacation he frequently took the duty at Buscot Parsonage, where Morris's friend Oswald Birchall was curate from 1878 and rector from 1884. Even Daniel's printing had its Morrisian connections; for in 1884, 1887 and again in 1888 he printed small volumes of poetry by Morris's undergraduate friend R.W. Dixon, with whom Morris had resumed his connection through George Howard in the mid-1870s. However the acquaintance between Morris and Daniel actually began, it culminated, as the Kelmscott Manor visitor book shows, in a visit by Daniel to Kelmscott in June 1892 (Sharp 1999, 47); and with the Kelmscott Press well under way at this point it is certainly likely that printing was high on the conversational agenda that day.

So Morris may well, after all, have known something of the Daniel Press, though when that knowledge began and whether it played any kind of formative role in prompting him towards his Kelmscott Press plans and projects we cannot say for sure. But what is clear, as Falconer Madan himself has pointed out, is that the motivation of Daniel's private press was fundamentally different from Morris's. The Daniel Press was a quietistic, inward-looking project, aimed at producing delightful books for a tiny circle of like-minded literary friends (only thirty-six copies of *The Garland of Rachel* were printed, for example). The Kelmscott Press had a much more robust and outward-directed mission: to boldly transform the overall quality of British printing and book production. So if the delicate Daniel volumes, with their Fell types, their seventeenth-century woodcut ornaments, their miniated capital letters and occasional needlework bindings by Mrs Daniel, did play any role in prompting Morris towards his Kelmscott project (and we cannot be sure of this), it was an Oxonian stimulus which was profoundly reworked and re-energised, as ever, as he responded to it. There is thus at least a possibility, *pace* William Peterson, that we must see an Oxford dimension to the Kelmscott Press beyond the formative role of the Bodleian Library on the young William Morris of the early 1850s.

Morris's address to the Oxford Socialist Union in October 1895 was 'a brilliant success in all ways' and it 'gives us a capital start', as the Union's secretary, J. Grenfell, bullishly reported (*Justice*, 9 November 1895, 6). It is not my purpose here to trace Oxford socialism in the years immediately after Morris's death in 1896. Yet it is worth noting that the Oxford Socialist Society had a representative at the London International Congress in that year (Kapp, II, 658) and that a vigorous, if contested, socialist agitation in Oxford continued thereafter. For as *The History of the University of Oxford* reports: 'Disruption of Socialist rallies at the Martyrs' Memorial in May and June of 1897 got out of hand when large crowds of undergraduates and local "roughs" joined forces to assault the speakers. The firing into the air of a revolver by a Wadham man, hardly to be overlooked even by Oxford's tolerant authorities, resulted in a ban on undergraduate attendance at such rallies' (VII, 1, 472). Morris's last Oxford speech in the Central Boys' School clearly had had a significant political impact, though it was not until the early twentieth century, with the arrival of G.D.H. Cole at the University, that his intellectual and political heritage would be picked up in any full sense.

Conclusion

'Take Oxford, for instance,' said I.

News from Nowhere (*CW*, XVI, 69)

I have tried to demonstrate in the preceding chapters how passionately in the 1880s and early 1890s William Morris sought to have an active cultural and political impact on the university and city in which he had spent his undergraduate years. He is no longer a passive eighteen-year-old *tabula rasa*, on whom Oxford inscribes its inspiring medieval messages, but rather a seasoned activist, first architectural, then political, who aims to provoke dynamic changes in the city, changes which ideally last beyond the punctual occasions of his various lectures there by the formation of groups of like-minded academics, residents and students. And yet his relation to the city and university, even in these mature years, was never going to be all one way. We need, therefore, to see it also as a dialectical process, whereby Morris the activist aims to transform Oxford, which, in its turn, reacts back upon him in new ways, and especially, as I shall suggest in this conclusion, in some of his key literary works of the later years. The first section will discuss the ways in which Oxford newly inscribes itself in certain key Morris fictions, and the second part will move forward historically to suggest something of the pattern of his influence there in the years beyond his death in 1896.

In Morris's prose romance *A Dream of John Ball* Will Green asks the time-travelling narrator, 'Hast thou seen Oxford, scholar?', and in so doing prompts perhaps Morris's most famous evocation of the medieval city he loved so much: 'a vision of grey-roofed houses and a long winding street and the sound of many bells'. It is a line every bit as memorable and as charged with regretful longing as Matthew Arnold's 'that sweet city with her dreaming spires' from 'The Scholar Gipsy'. Yet if we restore Morris's evocation to its full context we see that it is a more complex thing than Arnold's vision. For the narrator's full response to Will Green's question is: 'A vision of grey-roofed houses and a long winding street and the sound of many bells came over me at that word as I nodded "Yes" to him, my mouth full of salt pork and rye-bread; and then I lifted my pot and we made the clattering mugs kiss and I drank' (*CW*, XVI, 223). The elegiac vision is simultaneously ironised and grounded by the guzzling of food and drink that accompanies it. There is a physical robustness here, a sensuous earthiness, that we would hardly associate with the elusive, intangible figure of Arnold's Scholar, who may look fleetingly back at the line of festal light in Christ Church hall but certainly does not partake in such feasts. We may appropriately recall Burne-Jones's comment, in relation to the illustrations for the Kelmscott Chaucer, that Morris 'ever had more robust and daring parts' than Burne-Jones himself did (MacCarthy, 648), or than Matthew Arnold too for that matter.

What prompts Will Green's question to the narrator in the first place? How and why does Oxford suddenly come into this romance, which was serialised in *Commonweal* from 13 November 1886 to 22 January 1887? Once the question is posed by Will, the narrator certainly seems to be transformed into an Oxford scholar or 'gatherer of tales', and we may therefore wonder whether Morris's renewed involvement with Oxford, in the Democratic Federation and then Socialist League campaigns of 1883 to 1885, had not sharpened his medievalism to the point where the writing of *John Ball* became both possible and necessary to him. Indeed, we could see the text as a successful instance of that third or collaborative relationship between Morris and his old university which the Kelmscott Press *Douce Apocalypse* project might also have embodied. Paul Meier has stressed how important the Oxford School of History, particularly the work of Thorold Rogers, was to the making of Morris's political romance, so to this extent the author is in an 'undergraduate' relationship to Oxford again, gratefully receiving the intellectual treasures which it has to give him (Meier, I, 110). But this raw ideological material is then powerfully refashioned into the militant work that *A Dream of John Ball* so movingly is, so Morris is also clearly his dynamic activist self of the early 1880s, seeking to transform his Oxonian raw materials in a socialist direction, not simply to reproduce them. And if we do indeed take the process of composition to be a 'collaborative' one of this kind, then Will Green's question to the narrator about the grey city is the trace or scar in the surface of the text of the underlying principle of its construction.

I want to extend the account I have been offering of *A Dream of John Ball* to Morris's great utopian romance, *News from Nowhere*, serialised in *Commonweal* in 1890 and published in book form in 1891. For it seems that to its earliest reviewers *News from Nowhere* was a much more distinctively 'Oxford book' than it may appear to us now over a century later. Maurice Hewlett in the *National Review* referred to the book's narrator, William Guest, as 'the Oxford Student (new style)' (Faulkner, 348), perhaps implying that the *John Ball* narrator had been the Oxford Student (old style). In a review in the *Academy* Lionel Johnson linked *News from Nowhere* to Matthew Arnold, seeing Morris's Thames-side idyll in the later chapters of the book as a politicised version of Arnold's 'Scholar Gipsy': 'Like that other Oxford poet, who loved "the shy Thames shore," Mr. Morris consoles and heartens us' (Faulkner, 343) – as if the fugitive 'spark from Heaven' of Arnold's poem had become the full-blooded revolution of 1952 in Morris's utopia. *News from Nowhere* itself makes the link too. 'Look, there is a ferry!', cries Ellen on the upper Thames, at a location that may well be the Bablockhythe of Arnold's poem, and in this way Morris's utopia seeks to incorporate its Oxonian precursor (*CW*, XVI, 188). This reference is the answer to Paul Thompson's worry that Morris 'probably ... enjoyed Matthew Arnold's pastoral poems, though he never acknowledged their influence' (P. Thompson, 148)

Once alerted to the Oxford dimension of the text in this way we quickly come to see how pervasive such references are across Morris's post-revolutionary world – even before the characters embark up the Thames to Kelmscott Manor. Indeed, what we witness is something like the 'Oxfordisation' of space and society in the world of Nowhere. Morris and Co. had themselves tried out this strategy in a small way in some of their early decorative experiments. Thus, as Ann Dean points out, the layout of the Firm's windows at Selsley Church, near Stroud, 'is partly derived from the arrangement of the late 13th century windows in Merton College Chapel, Morris's favourite building in Oxford' (Dean, 12). But in a fictional utopia, unconstrained by present social realities, Morris can explore this Oxfordising strategy on the grand scale.

William Guest's first breakfast in utopia has a distinctly Oxonian feel to it; for 'as I was putting the first mouthfuls into my mouth, my eye caught a carved and gilded inscription on the panelling, behind what we should have called the High Table in an Oxford college hall' (*CW*, XVI, 15). As in *John Ball*, enthusiastic eating and Oxonian reference are here combined, true to the principles of Morris's holistic (rather than Matthew Arnold's cerebral) definition of 'culture'. The great hall of Hammersmith Guest House is structured along the lines of a college hall, which Morris had already evoked as a utopian model in an 1884 article in *Justice* entitled 'Why Not?' Noting that 'at the risk of being considered dreamers … it is important for us to try and raise our ideals of the pleasure of life', he turns to Oxbridge as a means for doing so. There is, he writes, 'no insuperable difficulty in the way of lodging people in airy rooms decently decorated, in providing their lodgings not only with good public cooking and washing rooms, but also with beautiful halls for the common meal and other purposes, as in the Colleges of Oxford and Cambridge, which it would be [a] pleasure merely to sit in' (*PW*, 24–25). The college hall metaphor takes us back beyond the privatised household of the bourgeois nuclear family to a genuinely communal experience of eating and socialising, though the fact that something resembling a High Table also features in the Hammersmith Guest House prompts us to wonder what hierarchies might still survive in the otherwise thoroughly egalitarian world of Morris's Nowhere.

If social space is 'Oxfordised', so too is labour in the new society. The first substantial instance of work we come across in Nowhere is the 'gang of men road-mending' which Dick and Guest encounter as they wend their way across London to the British Museum. This incident bears a double Oxford coding. At the explicit textual level, it is Oxonian in its youthful high spirits and athleticism; for 'there were about a dozen of them, strong young men, looking much like a boating party at Oxford would have looked like in the days I remembered, and not more troubled with their work' (*CW*, XVI, 47). An elite experience of energetic camaraderie is now diffused across society as a whole, though the Oxonian poet and critic Alfred Noyes has offered a sourly dissenting opinion on the appropriacy of Morris's boating party metaphor here: 'He compares the jollity of the gang of road-makers with that of the "eight" of Oxford oarsmen; but if he were a rowing man, he would know that even oarsmen are never particularly anxious to be "held up" by punts or boat-loads of trippers, and that their methods of helping these last along might not be loud, but would certainly be deep' (Noyes, 132).

But there is a further dimension of meaning to the road-making/ boating party episode. We now need to delve behind the surface of the text to what is surely a vivid echo of John Ruskin's Ferry Hinksey road-building venture of 1874, which inspired undergraduates such as Arnold Toynbee and Oscar Wilde to try their hand at socially useful manual labour. If, as I have suggested above, Toynbee was a significant opponent of revolutionary socialism in the early 1880s, he here finds himself politically forgiven and redeemed in the joyous Oxonian road-mending of Morris's utopia.

In the course of Old Hammond's long disquisitions in the British Museum on the history and underlying principles of the new society, we learn that Oxford as a place of learning 'has reverted to some of its best traditions; so you may imagine how far it is from its nineteenth-century position' (*CW*, XVI, 70). This is a welcome discovery, for both Guest and ourselves as readers, but Hammond's remark is also limiting in its stress on Oxford as a specific and defined locale; it misses that pervasive 'Oxfordisation' that I have noted at work elsewhere in the text. For this process is in the end so thoroughgoing that Oxford itself, as both city and university, is paradoxically no longer a necessary presence in *News from Nowhere*.

On the upper waters of the Thames, the travellers fall in with Henry Morsom, a lively and learned old man who seems to them to be a rural version of Old Hammond. Offered a lift further up the river, Morsom replies: 'I will go as far as Oxford with you … I want a book or two out of the Bodleian Library. I suppose you will sleep in the old city' (180). It is good to know that the whole population has become so careful of its cultural treasures that the Bodleian can afford to become a lending, rather than a purely reference, library. Any Nowherian, it seems, might be trusted to borrow Morris's beloved *Douce Apocalypse* for a week or two, which takes us a stage beyond that limited democratisation which a Kelmscott facsimile of the work would have represented. Morris's utopia thus finally fulfils the vision sketched in the article on 'Oxford' in the *Oxford and Cambridge Magazine* of April 1856, where students are indeed allowed to borrow books from the Bodleian. Yet despite this benign development, and despite the fact that Oxford has now returned to the original Platonic essence of itself after its Victorian fall from grace, Guest, Dick and Clara do not sleep in the old city. Why not?

Again we need to distinguish between overt and underlying textual logics. At the surface level, the utopian travellers do not stay overnight in Oxford because Dick Hammond, as leader of their expedition, hurries them on past it, so keen is he to get to work on the haymaking in the Kelmscott fields beyond. This impatience of Dick's belongs to that overvaluation of physical and undervaluation of mental labour which has characterised him from his disputes with Bob the weaver in the very opening chapters of *News from Nowhere* – though we must add in his defence that he does offer Guest a visit to Oxford, 'and my learned lecture on it', on their return journey down the river a fortnight later (167). But we may also wonder whether, beneath Dick's urgency about Kelmscott haymaking, Morris's own 'terror' of Oxford in 1881, with which I opened this book, is not still faintly operative here, not fully redeemed even in utopia itself. The 'city he never visited willingly now', May Morris called the dreaming spires; and even Morris's utopian re-making of England cannot, it seems, quite efface the pain and the scars. No doubt Magdalen Bridge has been narrowed again and the old statues put back in place on St Mary's spire, but even these developments only result in the utopian travellers skimming the edges of Oxford, rather than actually staying in the city.

More fundamentally, however, you do not need to visit Oxford when everything around you has been 'Oxfordised'; to stay in Oxford itself, under those circumstances, would be merely otiose. Though Old Hammond had put much emphasis on Oxford as a specific site, he is also alert to this wider process at work in Nowhere. Evoking the rural architecture of the new society for Guest, he remarks: 'where the houses are thinly scattered they run large, and are more like the old colleges than ordinary houses as they used to be' (73). As Guest and his fellows head upriver this is indeed what they find, as with Walter Allen's house, which is 'built round a quadrangle big enough to get plenty of sunshine in it' (164–5), or the later 'quite modern stone house – a wide quadrangle of one story, the buildings that made it being quite low' (191). In the architectural dreamscape that opens *A Dream of John Ball* a lone 'collegiate church' makes its appearance in the Wiltshire countryside, but in the rural landscapes of *News from Nowhere* an altogether more thorough 'collegisation' of architecture has taken place: 'nowhere do we find skyscrapers, but rather a style of architecture inspired by the nostalgia born of the quadrangles of Oxford' (Meier, II, 403).

Hence it is that, far from sleeping in the city as Henry Morsom had assumed, the travellers 'skirted Oxford by Oseney' (*CW*, XVI, 185), stopping briefly by the castle to put Morsom himself ashore. One of the great projects of the revolution in *News from Nowhere* is to undo the distinction between city and country, and in the new society London has therefore become a green, unhurried and spacious garden-city, while the country has been culturally revivified by a mass exodus from the towns in the early years of the new epoch. Such an unravelling of stark binary oppositions is also achieved, as we have seen, between Oxford and its wider society, with dining spaces modelled on college halls, manual labour organised as cheerily as boating parties, and buildings built in quadrangular style. Oxford as metaphor and model for the new society is almost as pervasive in *News from Nowhere* as the fourteenth century itself (and the two codes are very intimately allied). No need, then, to stay overnight in a place which has radiated powerfully outwards and refashioned the entire new culture. No need now to foment a 'new Oxford movement' when Oxford has become one of the underlying principles or energies of everyday life in the post-revolutionary world.

As a utopia, *News from Nowhere* dramatises the triumph of Morris's values and campaigns: socialism defeats capitalism in the revolution of 1952, handicrafts have mostly displaced machine-production in the fully developed new society, and, as we have seen, architecture and labour have been Oxfordised as part of these broader transformations. Yet Morris's actual experience of his Oxford campaign had largely been one of defeat: Magdalen Bridge had been widened, the local branch of the Socialist League had run into the sands after Charles Faulkner's stroke in 1888, the statues of St Mary's Church had been removed and replaced. Perhaps the greatest defeat and cruellest irony of all is that the William Morris who had most effect on the social and environmental fabric of Oxford in the twentieth century was the capitalist car manu-facturer, William R. Morris, later Lord Nuffield, not the socialist and architectural activist who is the subject of this book. Strictly speaking, Morris's only fully successful local 'campaign' in Oxford was his support in March 1879 for W.B. Richmond's candidacy for the Slade Professor-ship there (*CL*, I, 505–6).

It is therefore perhaps no accident that it is the narrator of *A Dream of John Ball* who has both the most evocative vision of Oxford and the most profound meditation on political defeat in all of Morris's work. The former I have cited above, the latter famously runs as follows: 'I pondered all these things, and how men fight and lose the battle, and the thing that they fought for comes about in spite of their defeat, and when it comes turns out not to be what they meant, and other men have to fight for what they meant under another name' (*CW*, XVI, 231–2). If Morris's own Oxonian campaigns – that sustained effort to kickstart a 'new Oxford movement', architectural and political – were mostly doomed to failure, we now need to ask briefly about how they subsisted there beyond his own lifetime, about the paradoxical ways in which they were picked up and fought for by 'other men' in the twentieth century.

The poet and critic Alfred Noyes, who went up to Morris's old college, Exeter, in 1898, wrote in his 1908 study of Morris in the 'English Men of Letters' series that it was in Oxford 'that his work has struck deep-est root. It is there that generation after generation of undergraduates reads the *Defence of Guenevere*, and covers its walls with reproductions

of his work and that of Burne-Jones' (Noyes, 13). Yet this evidence of
enduring influence would hardly have satisfied Morris himself, for it is
his poetic and decorative identity of the 1860s and early 1870s that is
essentially being celebrated here, as if the tougher architectural and
political Oxford campaign from 1879 to 1895 had never happened. If
this were indeed all that Morris had bequeathed to Oxford, along with
a few Kelmscott Press books in Exeter College library, then it would
have constituted a terminal defeat for the indefatigable socialist activist
of the 1880s.

Now clearly Morris's legacy did survive at Oxford in more robust
form than Noyes allows. Yet that survival remains paradoxical. For
while Morris himself could hold together literary, architectural and
political concerns, bringing them to an extraordinary synthesis in *News
from Nowhere*, these varied emphases tended to go their own ways in
early-twentieth-century Oxford. On the cultural side, Morris's architectural concerns have been taken up strongly within the city, but in
ways that no longer connect to a wider critique of society. His Icelandic,
Anglo-Saxon and romance-writing literary interests were energetically
developed at the University, above all by J.R.R. Tolkien, Rawlinson and
Bosworth Professor of Anglo-Saxon from 1924, but within the context of
a very different and non-Morrisian politics. On the explicitly political
front, G.D.H. Cole, who became Reader in Economics at Oxford in 1925,
sustained Morris's socialist values, but in ways that no longer fully
connected with the latter's cultural emphases. Architecture, literature
and politics had split asunder, or, to adapt T.S. Eliot's terminology, a
'dissociation of sensibility' had set in within Morris's Oxonian heritage
from which it has perhaps never fully recovered.

Early-twentieth-century Oxford had many defenders of its historic
urban fabric, some of them with direct links back to Morris's most
active years in the city. His former protégé, Edward Nicholson, published a pamphlet in 1910 entitled *Can We Not Save Architecture in
Oxford?*, pleading for the appointment of an architect as Slade Professor so that Oxford might avoid in the future the kind of disastrous
building errors it had made in the past. The Oxford Architectural and
Historical Society (which in Morris's undergraduate years met in the
Holywell Music Room) established an Old Houses Committee in 1912,

whose report lamented the demolition of Oxford's domestic architecture and contained photographs and notes on fourteen surviving buildings, including some of the houses in Holywell Street about which Morris himself had been so exercised (Whiting, 126). Most crucially, the Oxford Preservation Trust was formally launched at a meeting in the Sheldonian Theatre in October 1927, one of its main creators being the elderly Michael Sadler, who had enthusiastically attended Ruskin's lectures at Oxford as an undergraduate in the early 1880s and, as we have noticed above, had met Morris there during those years. Sadler's long and distinguished career in the university extension movement was one of the (non-revolutionary) directions in which the 'new Oxford movement' of the 1880s could subsequently find expression, and now, in his later years, he moved closer to the kind of SPAB-inspired campaigns which Morris had launched at Oxford in 1881 and 1893. The 'vulgarisation of Oxford' had certainly proceeded apace during the early twentieth century, and May Morris, reprinting in 1936 her father's 1885 reply to the *Daily News*, reflected ruefully that the letter 'is melancholy reading to-day for us who watch the steady progress of the vulgarization since his time' (*AWS*, I, 3). It would certainly be interesting to track down any further detail that survives regarding her responses to architectural developments in the city in these decades.

Like Frederick York Powell, J.R.R. Tolkien had discovered for himself in boyhood the literary works which meant so much to Morris in middle age. When Tolkien first read the story of Sigurd slaying the dragon Fafnir in Andrew Lang's *Red Fairy Book* he was drawn powerfully into its Northern imaginative world; 'I desired dragons with a profound desire', he later confessed (Carpenter 2002, 39). At King Edward's Grammar School, Birmingham, he plunged deeply into philology, learning Anglo-Saxon, reading widely in Middle English, even venturing into Old Norse so that he could read the Sigurd–Fafnir story in the original. In later school years he gave a paper to the Literary Society on the Norse Sagas, with readings in the original, and he would occasionally impress the Debating Society by breaking into fluent Gothic or Anglo-Saxon.

Tolkien went up to Exeter College in 1911 and in summer term 1913 switched from Classics to English, so that he could specialise in Old and Middle English and other Germanic languages; his special subject was

Old Norse, which led to wide reading in the sagas and Eddas. It was in 1914 that his encounter with William Morris finally came; for when he won the college's Skeat Prize for English in that year he spent the money on medieval Welsh texts and works by Morris: *The Life and Death of Jason*, his translation of the *Volsunga Saga*, and his prose-and-verse romance *The House of the Wolfings*. In the last text in particular, remarks Humphrey Carpenter in his lively biography of Tolkien, 'Morris's view of literature coincided with his own', to the point indeed that when Tolkien tried to versify the Finnish *Story of Kullervo* later that year he achieved 'little more than a pastiche of Morris' (99–100, 104).

We can see a double-sided influence at work here. If Morris's version of the Volsunga Saga helped confirm Tolkien in his Old Norse enthusiasms, his other writings opened up literary rather than scholarly possibilities. Hence it is that when in the post-Great War years Tolkien began work on the 'Book of Lost Tales' that was to become *The Silmarillion*, Morris's inspiration loomed large: the unifying device of a voyager hearing a sequence of tales may be borrowed from *The Earthly Paradise* (though Tolkien later abandoned it), and the style of 'The Fall of Gondolin', in Humphrey Carpenter's view, 'suggests that Tolkien was influenced by Morris' (Carpenter 2002, 129). More generally, Morris's series of late prose romances, from *The Wood beyond the World* onwards, clearly initiated that genre of adult fantasy to which *The Lord of the Rings* was later such a spectacular contribution.

When Tolkien returned to Oxford as Professor of Anglo-Saxon after a stint at Leeds he was determined to reform the English School in favour of early English and other early literatures. As part of this project he formed the 'Coalbiters' group in 1926, which aimed to read its way through the Icelandic sagas in the original; and by early 1927 C.S. Lewis, Fellow and Tutor in English at Magdalen College, was an enthusiastic member of the group. Friendship with Tolkien seems powerfully to have reactivated the Northern literary enthusiasms of Lewis's own boyhood, which Carpenter summarises as follows:

> He was delighted by the romances of William Morris. Best of all, he one day chanced across an Arthur Rackham illustration to *Siegfried and the Twilight of the Gods*, and felt the same sensation as he had known when he first read the Longfellow lines about Balder. 'Pure "Northernness"

engulfed me,' he said; and he began a quest for everything 'Northern'. Books of Norse myths, a synopsis of the *Ring* operas, Wagner's music itself, all were food to his imagination. Soon he was writing his own poem on the Nibelung story. (Carpenter 1997, 5)

Lewis, who had at first been hostile to Tolkien's syllabus reform proposals, noted in his diary that Tolkien 'thinks the language is the real thing in the school ... His pet abomination is the idea of "liberal studies"' (Carpenter 1997, 22–3). Such views are clearly very close to those advanced by Morris himself in his 1886 letter to the *Pall Mall Gazette* about literary studies at Oxford, where he had argued, as we have seen, that 'philology can be taught, but "English Literature" cannot'. Morris had there complained that a Professor of Literature would probably begin the subject with Shakespeare rather than *Beowulf*, and it was just such a decisive reorientation back towards Anglo-Saxon and medieval texts, particularly at the expense of Victorian literature, that Tolkien and Lewis (once he had been won over) were struggling to effect in the late 1920s. Students on the modern or literary side of the School would give a lot more time to early period texts, with post-1830 literature lopped off to create space for this, and students on the language side of the syllabus could focus entirely on early literature without being compelled to study later authors; Icelandic too was given a good deal more prominence. After a long campaign in which, as Lewis colourfully put it, 'there are disguised orcs behind every tree', the Tolkien reforms were at last accepted by the Oxford English School in 1931 (Carpenter 2002, 195). Forty-five years later, then, English studies at Oxford had moved significantly back towards the kind of position Morris himself had sketched out in his 1886 response to the Churton Collins campaign.

In Morris himself, and in a much lesser way in Fredrick York Powell, Icelandic literary enthusiasms and socialist politics are closely bound together. But this was certainly not the case for the Rawlinson and Bosworth Professor of Anglo-Saxon. Tolkien was anti-democratic through and through. He supported Franco's fascists in the Spanish Civil War, and his ideal society was one ordered into 'estates'; he once memorably remarked that 'touching your cap to the Squire may be damn bad for the Squire but it's damn good for you' (Carpenter 2002, 174). C.S. Lewis's politics were only a touch more congenial. He maintained that democracy was only necessary because of the Fall (otherwise a patri-archal monarchy would have been his preferred mode of government), and he regarded the post-1945 Labour government under Clement Attlee as, in Humphrey Carpenter's phrase, 'the very devils of Hell incarnate' (Carpenter 1997, 206).

For the development of the political side of Morris's legacy at Oxford in the twentieth century, we need to look elsewhere entirely and turn to the socialist theorist G.D.H. Cole. In 1952 Cole declared that at the age of sixteen in 1905 he had been 'converted, quite simply, by reading William Morris's *News From Nowhere*, which made me feel, suddenly and irrevocably, that there was nothing except a Socialist that it was possible for me to be' (Wright, 14); and in later years he kept a bust of Morris in his library. Thus throughout Cole's voluminous political writings it remains the case, as Anthony Wright has demonstrated in a fine recent study, that 'fellowship … as expressed in the sort of social relationships described in *News from Nowhere*, stood as the key socialist principle, from which all other principles were derived' (271).

Yet the influence of Morris could lead in various directions, and in Cole's schoolboy days 'it was the impact of Morris's romantic verse that was decisive, leading Cole towards literary criticism and poetic creation' (15), though not to the Anglo-Saxon and Icelandic enthusiasms of the young Tolkien. So that when Cole arrived in Oxford as a student in 1908 and founded the journal *The Oxford Socialist* it was an effusive and lyrical vision of brotherhood that underpinned his vision. Unable to define a political vehicle of its own, this bold poetic vision of fellow-ship paradoxically attached itself to the dryly permeationist tactics of Fabianism, of which in these early years Cole strongly approved.

It was the sudden, intense militancy of the pre-war years – Irish, feminist and above all industrial – which energised Cole towards the formation of his own distinctive politics in which Morris would have a new meaning for him. He responded strongly to the appeal of syn-dicalism, which he saw as a necessary reassertion of the producers' viewpoint, and in a set of papers to the Oxford Fabians in 1912, the year in which he was elected to a prize fellowship at Magdalen College, he began to distance himself from Fabian collectivism: 'it had forgotten the need to make the workplace the arena of a joyful creativity … The essential meaning of Morris, for example, was now seen no longer in terms of an epic romanticism but crucially in terms of the recognition that freedom and self-determination in the workplace were the key to a wider self-expression' (22). Fellowship in the workplace clearly had sharper political implications than fellowship as a benign universal principle, and Cole was now – as he involved himself in the celebrated Oxford tram strike of 1913 – on the verge of formulating a Morrisian politics for the early twentieth century.

One further necessary stage came through Cole's involvement with the *New Age*, which under the editorship of A.R. Orage had been developing the 'Guild' vision of the Ruskin-inspired architect A.J. Penty. Guild Socialism was not Cole's invention, but he was to run with the idea and became its best-known spokesperson, purging the movement of its medievalist and Christian Socialist dimensions in the process. Guild Socialism took on board what seemed valuable in syndicalism, interpreting industrial unrest as the expression of an instinct for workers' participation, but went beyond syndicalism in its vision of a genuine partnership between centralised state and decentralised trade unions or 'guilds' (although there would be controversies over the exact nature of this partnership within the movement). As Wright argues, 'From Rousseau and Morris in their different ways, Cole developed his conception of a community founded upon the cooperation of self-governing associations' (24). 'The Guild System will bring Morris into his own', Cole insisted in *Self-Government in Industry* in 1917, 'under Collectivism, he would be remembered only as a quite unpractical Socialist who was so little "in the swim" that he refused to join the Fabian Society' (Cole, 210). Cole and other *New Age* contributors formed the National Guilds League in 1915 as a political movement to press forward the Guild Socialist agenda.

Cole's subsequent life's work at Oxford was politically variable. In 1925 he was appointed to the new position of Reader in Economics and also became a Fellow of University College. Whether we can consider him as a worthy socialist successor to Charles Faulkner there is a moot point, however, for in *The Next Ten Years in British Social and Economic Policy* (1929), Cole retracted many of his early Guild Socialist commitments. However, after the fall of the MacDonald government he began to move back to the left again, and on his appointment to the Chichele Professorship of Social and Political Theory in 1944 he was once more taking up the cudgels against statism and speaking out on behalf of the pluralism of his earlier days. It is, then, Guild Socialism, with its vision of a creative and self-managed labour process and of a federation of self-governed communities, which remains Cole's lasting development of the Morris legacy at Oxford.

For all the passion that William Morris put into his Oxford campaigns over the years, he never did succeed in creating the new Oxford movement which some of his contemporaries thought likely to emerge in the early 1880s. Later commentators have been much more sceptical about the very possibility of such a new formation emerging, with Janet Howarth arguing that 'the diverse origins of Oxford's interests in social questions [in the 1880s] guaranteed that they would never form the basis of a movement' (*HUO*, VII, 2, 642). And in many ways, as I have shown, Morris's Oxford experience was one of defeat: architecturally over Magdalen Bridge and St Mary's Church, politically as the Oxford Socialist League foundered after 1888.

A poignant final image of this is afforded by Morris's encounter with two Oxford men on his last-ditch medical trip to Norway in July–August 1896. With one of them, a Mr Taylor, he had 'many animated discussions on literary subjects', as John Carruthers reported to May Morris in 1913; but as regards the other, Dr George Brodrick, a senior representative of official Oxford culture, Morris had more reservations: 'the super-Oxonian superiority of the Master of Merton was the subject of a few quiet jokes' (MacCarthy, 666). Whether Morris tried to convert the Master of Merton to socialism on this trip, as William Hines had once tried with the Master of Balliol or Charles Faulkner with his Norwegian skipper, we do not know (in one sense, though, Morris already had tried, since Brodrick had attended his 'Art under Plutocracy' lecture in November 1883). He would certainly have had his work cut out. Brodrick, who had himself been tutored by Benjamin Jowett, was a high-profile university Liberal (and later Liberal Unionist), and, with a family estate of 9,580 acres and a Pall Mall apartment in London, he was by 1900 describing socialism as 'the most pernicious, while it is the most demonstrably false, delusion of our age' (Brodrick, 379). One's impression of the encounter, then, is of Oxonian social privilege and arrogance basically untouched, despite Morris's long campaign against it, whilst the campaigner himself, physically exhausted and close to death, is about to fade from the scene altogether as William Guest does eventually from the threshold of Kelmscott Church in *News from Nowhere.* Morris in fact died two months later, on 3 October 1896.

But if William Morris did not create an actual movement, he has at least created an enduring possibility at Oxford, an inspiring model for the ways in which culture – whether this be architecture, arts and crafts, or Icelandic literature – and politics can come fruitfully together in a socialist synthesis. I have argued in this conclusion that in the early twentieth century key elements of the Morrisian synthesis survived at Oxford but in ways that no longer fruitfully interacted. The Oxford Preservation Society sustained his conservationist impulse, Tolkien and Lewis sustained his medieval, Anglo-Saxon and Icelandic enthusiasms, and G.D.H. Cole developed the model of a decentralised Guild Socialism; but these are now – to adapt Theodor Adorno's great phrase – the torn elements of an integral freedom to which, however, they do not add up. Morris once remarked that 'Oxford taught me the need of beauty; Stepney taught me the need of humanity' (Stringer, 129); but as I have tried to demonstrate in this book, his Oxford campaign in later life came about when he undertook to teach Oxford rather than be taught by it – to teach it the need of both 'humanity' towards its own architectural heritage and passionate concern for the wider society in which it was such a privileged enclave. Whenever culture and politics come together again at Oxford the Morrisian 'possibility' has been reactivated, as it no doubt will be again in the twenty-first century, though in utopian shapes which we as yet can perhaps not imagine. For this 'intransigent son of a somewhat "disobedient" mother', as May Morris once memorably characterised her father's relation to Oxford, still has the capacity to rouse the city and university he both loved and hated (*CW*, XI, xv).

Bibliography

Ashley, M.P., and C.T. Saunders, *Red Oxford: A History of the Growth of Socialism in the University of Oxford*, 2nd edn (Oxford: Oxford Labour Club, 1933).

Bacon, Alan, 'Deliver Us from Two (or more) Professors of Criticism', *Journal of the William Morris Society*, vol. IX, no. 1, Autumn 1990, 29–34.

Ball, Oonan Howard, *Sidney Ball: Memories and Impressions of an Ideal Don* (Oxford: Basil Blackwell, 1923).

Beerbohm, Max, *And Even Now* (London: William Heinemann, 1922 [1920]).

Betjeman, John, and David Vaisey, *Victorian and Edwardian Oxford from Old Photographs* (London: Batsford, 1971).

Boos, Florence, ed., *William Morris's Socialist Diary* (London: Journeyman Press, 1982).

Brodrick, George C., *Memories and Impressions* (London: James Nisbet, 1900).

Burne-Jones, Georgiana, *Memorials of Edward Burne-Jones*, 2 vols (London: Macmillan, 1912).

Carpenter, Humphrey, *J.R.R. Tolkien: A Biography* (London: HarperCollins, 2002).

Carpenter, Humphrey, *The Inklings: C.S. Lewis, J.R.R. Tolkien, Charles Williams and Their Friends* (London: HarperCollins, 1997).

Case, Thomas, *St. Mary's Clusters: An Historical Enquiry concerning the Pinnacled Steeple of the University Church, Oxford, with Illustrations* (Oxford: James Parker, 1893).

Cole, G.D.H., *Self-Government in Industry* (London: Hutchinson, 1972 [1917]).

Cook, E.T., and Alexander Wedderburn, *The Works of John Ruskin*, 37 vols (London: George Allen, 1903–12).

Dean, Ann S., *Burne-Jones and William Morris in Oxford and the Surrounding Area* (Malvern: Heritage Press, rev. edn, 1996).

Dunlap, Joseph, *The Book that Never Was* (New York: Oriole Editions, 1971).

Edinburgh University Socialist Society, *Beauty for Ashes: An Appeal* (Edinburgh, 1884).

Ellis, F.S., 'The Life-Work of William Morris', *Journal of the Society of Arts*, vol. 46, part 2375, 27 May 1898, 618–28.

Elton, Oliver, *Frederick York Powell: A Life*, 2 vols (Oxford: Clarendon Press, 1906).

Faulkner, Peter, ed., *William Morris: The Critical Heritage* (London: Routledge & Kegan Paul, 1973).

Graham, Malcolm, *The Suburbs of Victorian Oxford: Growth in a Pre-industrial City*, Ph.D. thesis, University of Leicester, 1985.

Grylls, Rosalie Glynn, *Portrait of Rossetti* (London: Macdonald, 1964).

Gwynne, Stephen, *Experiences of a Literary Man* (London: Thornton Butterworth, 1926).

Harvie, Christopher, *The Lights of Liberalism: University Liberals and the Challenge of Democracy 1860–86* (London: Allen Lane, 1976).

Henderson, Philip, *William Morris: His Life, Work and Friends* (London: Thames & Hudson, 1967).

Hilton, Tim, *John Ruskin* (New Haven: Yale University Press, 2002).

Hinchcliffe, Tanis, *North Oxford* (New Haven: Yale University Press, 1992).

Hope, Anthony, *Memories and Notes* (London: Hutchinson, 1927).

Horn, P.L.R., 'The Farm Workers, the Dockers and Oxford University', *Oxoniensia*, vol. 32, 1967, 60–70.

Hunter, Michael, ed., *Preserving the Past: The Rise of Heritage in Modern Britain* (Stroud: Alan Sutton, 1996).

Hyndman, H.M., *The Record of an Adventurous Life* (New York: Garland, 1984 [1911]).

Jackson, Thomas Graham, *The Church of St. Mary the Virgin, Oxford* (Oxford: Clarendon Press, 1897).

Jackson, Thomas Graham, *Recollections: The Life and Travels of a Victorian Architect*, ed. Sir Nicholas Jackson (London: Unicorn Press, 2003).

Jackson, William Walrond, *Ingram Bywater: The Memoir of an Oxford Scholar 1840–1914* (Oxford: Clarendon Press, 1917).

Jones, Peter d'A., *The Christian Socialist Revival, 1877–1914: Religion, Class and Social Conscience in late-Victorian England* (Princeton, NJ: Princeton University Press, 1968).

Kadish, Alon, *Apostle Arnold: The Life and Death of Arnold Toynbee, 1852–1883* (Durham, NC: Duke University Press, 1968).

Kapp, Yvonne, *Eleanor Marx*, 2 vols (London: Virago, 1979).

Lago, Mary, ed., *Burne-Jones Talking* (London: John Murray, 1981).

LeMire, Eugene, *The Unpublished Lectures of William Morris* (Detroit: Wayne State University Press, 1969).

MacCarthy, Fiona, *William Morris: A Life for Our Time* (London: Faber & Faber, 1994).

MacColl, D.S., postcard to Sydney Cockerell, 10 November 1944, *Cockerell Papers*, vol. CXI, British Library Add. MS. 52733.

MacColl, D.S., letter to Sydney Cockerell, 25 September 1945, *Cockerell Papers*, vol. CXI, British Library Add. MS. 52733.

Mackail, J.W., *The Life of William Morris*, 1899, 2 vols bound as one (New York: Dover, 1995).

Madan, F., ed., *The Daniel Press: Memorials of C.H.O. Daniel* (London: Wm Dawson, 1974 [1921–2]).

Mearns, Andrew, *The Bitter Cry of Outcast London*, ed. Anthony S. Wohl (Leicester: Leicester University Press, 1970).

Meier, Paul, *William Morris: The Marxist Dreamer*, 2 vols, trans. Frank Gubb (Hassocks: Harvester Press, 1978).

Morris, William, 'Annual Report of the SPAB – V', 1882, William Morris Internet Archive, www.marxists.org/archive/morris/index.htm.

Morris, William, 'What We Have to Look For', 30 March 1895, British Library Add. MS. 45333[3].

Nicholson, Edward Williams Byron, *Can We Not Save Architecture in Oxford?* (Oxford: Henry Frowde, 1910).

Noyes, Alfred, *William Morris* (London: Macmillan, 1908).

'Oxford', anon., *Oxford and Cambridge Magazine*, no. 4, April 1856, 234–57.

Peterson, William S., *The Kelmscott Press: A History of William Morris's Typographical Adventure* (Oxford: Oxford University Press, 1991).

Pinkney, Tony, ed., *We Met Morris: Interviews with William Morris, 1885–96* (Reading: Spire Books, 2005).

Quiller-Couch, Arthur, *Memories and Opinions: An Unfinished Autobiography*, ed. S.C. Roberts (Cambridge: Cambridge University Press, 1945).

'Recollections of William Morris', anon., *Artist*, vol. 20, 1897, 61–3.

Richter, Melvin, *The Politics of Conscience: T.H. Green and His Age* (London: Weidenfeld & Nicolson, 1964).

Sadleir, Michael, *Michael Sadler: A Memoir by His Son* (London: Constable, 1949).

Samuel, Rt Hon. Viscount, *Memoir* (London: Cresset Press, 1945).

Salmon, Nicholas, with Derek Baker, *The William Morris Chronology* (Bristol: Thoemmes Press, 1996).

Sharp, Frank, 'A Lesson in International Relations: Morris and the SPAB', *Journal of the William Morris Society*, vol. X, no. 2, Spring 1993, 9–15.

Sharp, Frank, 'William Morris's Kelmscott Connections', *Journal of the William Morris Society*, vol. XII, no. 2, Spring 1999, 44–53.

Stansky, Peter, *Redesigning the World: William Morris, the 1880s, and the Arts and Crafts* (Princeton, NJ: Princeton University Press, 1985).

Stringer, Arthur, 'William Morris as I Remember Him', *Craftsman*, vol. 4, part 2, May 1903, 25–32.

Super, R.H., ed., *The Complete Prose Works of Matthew Arnold*, 10 vols (Ann Arbor: University of Michigan Press, 1960–74).

Thompson, E.P., *William Morris: Romantic to Revolutionary* (New York: Pantheon, 1977).

Thompson, Paul, *The Work of William Morris* (London: Heinemann, 1967).

Vallance, Aymer, *The Life and Work of William Morris*, 1897 (London: Studio Editions, 1995).

Venning, Philip, 'Back to the Battle: 1881–1882: Magdalen Bridge, Oxford', *Cornerstone: The Magazine of the Society for the Protection of Ancient Buildings*, vol. 26, no. 3, 2005, 25.

Vincent, Andrew, 'Green, Thomas Hill (1836–1882)', *Oxford Dictionary of National Biography*, ed. H.C.G. Matthew and Brian Harrison, vol. 23 (Oxford: Oxford University Press, 2004), 534–40.

Whiting, R.C., ed., *Oxford: Studies in the History of a University Town since 1800* (Manchester: Manchester University Press, 1993).

Williams, Raymond, *Culture and Society: 1780–1950* (London: Chatto & Windus, 1958).

Wright, Anthony, *G.D.H. Cole and Socialist Democracy* (Oxford: Clarendon Press, 1979).

Index